You grab the dropped machine-gun and open fire, cutting down the remaining guard. Climbing to your feet, you gaze around the yard, searching for signs of any further trouble.

Suddenly, two Germans run from a building on the other side of the yard. Reacting without thinking, you swing the machine-gun and cut them down.

Only seconds have passed, but both Germans lie dead. Suddenly you hear the sound of a rifle being cocked and then, "Hande Hoch!" from behind you.

Dropping your weapon, you turn and see a scared soldier facing you with a machine-gun in his unsteady hands.

The HQ is in turmoil. Germans appear from every direction; a red-faced officer strides up to you and snaps, "For this you will be shot, Britischer!"

REAL LIFE GAMEBOOKS
THE GREAT ESCAPE

SIMON FARRELL AND JON SUTHERLAND

ILLUSTRATED BY BRIAN WILLIAMS

BERKLEY BOOKS, NEW YORK

To Brian Degas

This book was originally published in England
under the title THROUGH THE WIRE.

This Berkley / Pacer book contains the complete
text of the original hardcover edition.

THE GREAT ESCAPE

A Berkley/Pacer book, published by arrangement
with André Deutsch Limited

PRINTING HISTORY
André Deutsch edition published 1986
Berkley/Pacer edition / April 1988

ISBN: 0-425-10922-4
RL: 9.5

Pacer is a trademark belonging to
The Putnam Publishing Group.

A BERKLEY BOOK ® TM 757,375
Berkley/Pacer books are published by The Berkley Publishing Group,
200 Madison Avenue, New York, NY 10016.
The name "BERKLEY" and the "B" logo
are trademarks belonging to Berkley Publishing Corporation.

10   9   8   7   6   5   4   3   2   1

REAL LIFE GAMEBOOKS

This is a new kind of role-playing gamebook. *Real Life Gamebooks* take you into the past and allow you to experience great moments in history for yourself. You become a character of the time, faced with a series of important decisions which plunge you deep into the events and life of the period. You will meet and talk with major historical figures and become privy to their thoughts and actions, perhaps even influence their decisions yourself!

Think carefully before you make your choices. Danger waits for the unwary in these troubled times and the wrong decision could mean the end of your adventure before it has properly begun.

There are instructions on how to play *Real Life Gamebooks* (you will need a pencil, an eraser and two six-sided dice or the Random Number Table on page 17), a description of the events which are taking place in the world at the time, and a full personal background about your character and what may be expected of you.

You may not complete the story first time; you may wish to go back and try again, seeing what would happen if you made different choices. So make a Character Sheet for yourself on a piece of paper, based on the example on page 14. When you want to have another try all you have to do is make up a new Character Sheet.

EUROPE IN THE 1940's

In many ways World War II was a continuation of the 1914–18 war. The Germans, led by their dictator Adolf Hitler, were determined to wipe out the shame of their defeat at the hands of the Allies. Germany reoccupied the Rhineland in 1936; in 1938 she annexed Austria; and in two stages in 1938 and 1939 she occupied virtually all of Czechoslovakia. Apart from making verbal protests, no country tried to stop her. Then, on September 1 1939, Germany invaded Poland. Two days later Great Britain and France at last declared war.

Poland fell, and for the next six months things were very quiet, so much so that people began to call it a phoney war. But in April 1940, the hammer struck again. Denmark was taken almost totally by surprise, and Norway surrendered in June, despite British intervention.

On May 10, Germany moved on the west; she overran the Netherlands in four days, and Belgium in three weeks. France herself fell in just seven weeks. The British Expeditionary Force of 250,000 men made a valiant fighting retreat to Dunkirk, to be rescued quite amazingly by an armada of small boats.

Britain now stood alone, with the threat of immediate German invasion hanging over her head. All that Germany needed to do was to destroy the Royal Air Force . . .

The Second World War

1939

1 September: Germany invades Poland.

3 September: Britain and France declare war on Germany.

1940

9 April: Germany invades Denmark and Norway.

24 May: Germany invades France.

27 May: Britain begins to evacuate troops from Dunkirk.

July–September: Battle of Britain – British air victory prevents German invasion.

1941

22 June: Germany invades Russia.

7 December: Japan launches air attack on US Pacific Fleet at Pearl Harbor, Hawaii.

8 December: USA and Britain declare war on Japan.

1942

15 February: Japan captures Singapore.

6 September: Battle of Stalingrad: Germans defeated.

23 October: Battle of El Alamein: German troops under Rommel defeated by Allies.

1943

31 January: Remains of German army outside Stalingrad surrender to Russians.

1 July: USA begins to recapture the Japanese-held islands in the Pacific.

1944

4 June: Allied troops reach Rome.

6 June: D-Day landings in Normandy.

25 August: Paris is liberated.

1945

25 April: Russian troops surround Berlin.

27 April: American and Russian troops meet up at Torgau, Germany.

30 April: Hitler commits suicide.

7 May: Germany surrenders. End of the war in Europe.
6 and 9 August: Atomic bombs dropped on Japanese cities.
14 August: Japan surrenders. World War II ends.

REAL LIFE GAMEBOOK RULES

THE SEVEN SKILLS

There are seven main types of skill in which a character would be proficient in these turbulent times. The degree of ability in any one of these skills will fall between 2 (the worst) and 12 (the best).

The choice of skills is entirely up to you. To start the game you are given a pool of 50 skill points which you can allocate amongst the seven skills. You must give at least 2 points to each of them, and you may not give more than 12 to any one.

The skills in *Through the Wire* are: Pilot, Agility, Luck, Persuasion, Firearm, Language and Driving. Read the information about each skill below and examine the sample character at the end of this section before you allocate your points and fill in the totals on your Character Sheet.

Pilot: – Since your character is a fighter pilot in the Battle of Britain, he will be faced with both difficult aerial manoeuvres and dangerous enemy pilots. He will need to give and receive orders over the R/T (Radio Telephone), keep an eye open for approaching aircraft and watch for danger to other pilots of his squadron – all at the same time.

Agility: – This skill enables your character to avoid dangerous situations by leaping out of windows, dodging bullets or diving for cover.

Luck: – In certain situations, the only option you will have is to place your character's life in the hands of fate. It is often useful to be very lucky!

Persuasion: – In sticky circumstances you will need to be able to talk your way out of a problem. If you are caught cold with no weapon and nowhere to run, a bit of gentle persuasion will often pay off.

Firearm: – Although your character would not ordinarily be required to be a particularly good shot, you never know when this might come in handy. This skill covers all weapons from pistols to heavy machine guns.

Language: – This skill enables your character to converse at your choice of fluency in the common European languages – such as French and German. English is of course taken for granted.

Driving: – This skill gives your character the ability to drive any type of vehicle, from a motorbike to a tank.

HOW THE SKILLS WORK

Combat

There will be times in the course of the adventure when your character will have to fight. Although this can almost always be avoided by making the correct choices, it is not always to your advantage to run from combat. In such cases, the paragraph at which the fight takes place will give you all the information you need. You will be told three things: What weapon you must use (if you have a choice, you will be told so), what kind of opponent you are facing, and which numbered paragraphs to turn to if you are victorious or if you are beaten.

Your opponent will be described like this:

Sentry   Rifle 7

When you make your Character Sheet, you should also make a number of Combat Boxes (examples given on page 15). Each time you are about to enter a fight, you should use one of these Combat Boxes to fill in the details about yourself and your opponent. This is particularly useful if you are fighting more than one foe. Most importantly do not forget to write down the number of the paragraph where the fight is taking place.

The way you decide the outcome of the battle is simple. Throw two dice, and if the number you roll is *equal to or less than* your own skill score then you have hit and killed your opponent. If you have no dice, use the Random Number Table on page 17 and follow the instructions on its use.

Once you have rolled the dice for your own attack, you must do the same for your opponent(s). If the number you roll is *equal to or less than* his skill score, he hits you.

The battle continues in this way, with you rolling the dice for yourself and your opponent alternately, until either you or he is killed.

In some cases you automatically get the first shot, at other times your opponent(s) will shoot first. If it is not stated in the paragraph, you fire first.

Other Skills

In the course of your adventure, there will be times when you must use some of your other skills. For example, you may need to talk your way past a sentry (Persuasion skill), or you may need to try your luck in a sticky situation.

Whenever you are asked to test any of your other skills, you must throw two dice and try to roll a number *equal to or less than* your score in that particular skill. If you have no dice, use the Random Number Table on page 17 and follow the instructions on its use. If you succeed, you will be asked to turn to one paragraph. If you fail, you will have to turn to a different one.

Sometimes you will have to make rolls to test several different skills to accomplish a task.

SAMPLE CHARACTER

Pilot:	12	Watch out Black Baron, you are up against a killer pilot!
Agility:	7	Nowhere near Olympic standard, but this character would not fall over his own feet.
Luck:	8	Reasonably high. Quite a lucky character.
Persuasion:	8	Quite a smooth talker, but don't rely too heavily on the gift of the gab!

Firearm:	8	Not quite an expert, but should hit things more often than not.
Language:	4	No teacher would have let this character take a GCSE in French. He wouldn't have stood a chance.
Driving:	3	This is the sort of character who would have failed his driving test at least eight times before being given it for perseverance alone.

Copy the Sample Character Sheet over the page (page 14) on a piece of paper and fill it in in pencil, so that you can rub out the totals and use the sheet you have made another time. You don't have to copy the skill points given in the Sample Character Sheets; you can decide for yourself how many points you want for each skill, as long as they add up to 50.

Do the same with the Combat Boxes shown on page 15. You may well need as many as eight Combat Boxes before your adventure ends.

CHARACTER SHEET

SKILLS	RATINGS (2–12)
Pilot	12
Agility	6
Luck	8
Persuasion	7
Firearm	4
Language	4
Driving	9

COMBAT BOXES

Paragraph you came from: Your Skill: Opponent's:	Paragraph you came from: Your Skill: Opponent's:
Paragraph you came from: Your Skill: Opponent's:	Paragraph you came from: Your Skill: Opponent's:
Paragraph you came from: Your Skill: Opponent's:	Paragraph you came from: Your Skill: Opponent's:
Paragraph you came from: Your Skill: Opponent's:	Paragraph you came from: Your Skill: Opponent's:

Is the Past as exciting to you as it is to us?

If it is, then let us know. Tell us who your favourite character is, the period you would most like to have an adventure in and why. Send your letter to Simon Farrell and Jon Sutherland, Real Life Game Books, André Deutsch Limited, 105–106 Great Russell Street, London WC1B 3LJ.

REAL LIFE GAME BOOKS RANDOM NUMBER TABLE

If you do not have access to any six-sided dice, you may use this table instead. Simply place the book open in front of you and close your eyes. Point with your pencil until you touch the page and then open your eyes to read what number you have 'rolled'.

If any paragraph asks you for a number between one and six, then repeat the above instructions, but halve the number you 'roll', rounding down.

RANDOM NUMBER TABLE

10	7	11	4	7	9	9	5	4	12	10	8
5	5	6	3	6	10	7	7	8	8	7	3
6	8	11	7	9	5	2	4	8	6	6	9
11	6	7	11	8	3	5	7	10	6	12	9
7	9	7	3	10	6	5	4	8	8	7	5
6	6	9	8	2	10	5	4	8	7	4	9
5	4	8	9	7	7	7	8	6	12	5	6
7	11	8	6	4	7	8	3	9	2	8	7
5	6	11	9	9	3	10	4	6	5	10	10

PERSONAL BACKGROUND

Your name is Alistair Thompson and you are a Flight Officer in the Royal Air Force. The date is September 1940.

You have been literally living on Biggin Hill air field for the past two months, continually on stand-by. Every time the siren wails, at least three times a day, you leap into the cockpit of your aircraft.

The Luftwaffe, flying mostly Messerschmidts (Me109s) and Dorniers, have stepped up their attacks and, despite their heavy casualties, are gradually wearing your squadron down.

Only four months ago, you were a newcomer to the squadron; in the last few months you have seen many good pilots die horribly. Now you are an expert amongst the newcomers.

Each time you go up, you think it will be your last. The seemingly never-ending round of snatched sleep, bolted food, diesel fumes and the deafening roar of cannons and Merlin engines are gradually wearing you down.

One afternoon, during a brief lull in the chaos, your mind moves to thoughts of your home and family. They must have been evacuated from London by now; the last time you spoke they were on the point of going. Heaven help anyone still in the capital. You've intercepted dozens of attacks, but dozens more have got through unmolested to drop their bombs on the city.

'Scramble, scramble . . . scramble, scramble,' blares the loudspeaker.

Automatically you rise to your feet, donning your kit as you sprint towards your waiting Spitfire in red wing. In minutes you are in the air, flying high over the green fields of southern England, in search of unwanted visitors . . .

Now go to **1**.

1

'Hello, Red Leader, Control here. Bandits crossing coast over Dover. Vector 62.'

'Roger. Red Leader calling Squadron Six-two. Climb to 20,000, V formation. Keep the R/T clear please, gentlemen.'

'Yellow Leader calling Red Leader. Bandits 2 o'clock below.'

'Red Leader here, message understood. Control – one hundred plus bandits, half Dorniers, half Messerschmidts, six miles out, moving north-north-west. Making attack now.

'Red Leader to squadron. Formation attack. Choose your own targets, gentlemen.'

Ahead and below is a stream of German aircraft. Will you engage the fighter escort (go to **110**) or will you head for the bombers (go to **60**)?

2

An official military enquiry is held upon your release. But to your amazement, the line of questioning seems to be aimed at pinning the blame on you! You are the least well-known of the team, and the most likely suspect.

You must make a successful Persuasion skill roll to convince your questioners that they are wrong. If you succeed, turn to **292**. If not, turn to **20**.

3

The three other guards have not appeared – presumably they have wandered off into the undergrowth to relieve themselves. There are eight of you prisoners and only two guards. Will you decide to make the first move (go to **226**) or will you wait for someone else to do it (go to **95**)?

4

'We are bound for Calais, to see our uncle. We intend to stay here for the night,' you reply.

'I see, M'sieur. Your papers are in order, but you will have to find a hotel soon, curfew is at 7.00 P.M.,' he says.

'Merci, M'sieur,' you thank him.

Breathing a sigh of relief you leave the station and start walking along the main street of the town. Something tells you that all is not well and, glancing around, you see two men several yards behind you. You cross the road; they cross the road. You stop; they stop. You are being followed.

Will you run for it (go to **196**) or will you split up and meet each other later (go to **11**)?

5

The countryside is totally open. There is no cover at all. Just ahead, driving at speed along a track, is a Kubelwagon, a German staff car. In it are four soldiers, one driving, two with rifles and a third manning a machine-gun mounted on the top. Will you run for it (go to **141**) or will you surrender (go to **37**)?

6

The headlight moves across the bush you are hiding behind, then back again, as the German by the motorbike screams to his companion. You have been seen! Will you run for it (go to **141**) or will you surrender (go to **37**)?

7

You cross the road safely and head off vaguely southwest. The darkness is beginning to lift, so you had better find somewhere to hide for the day. Ahead is a farm and as you approach it you can see that the farmer has already begun milking. Keeping out of sight you slip into one of his barns and hide in the hayloft. Now go to **193**.

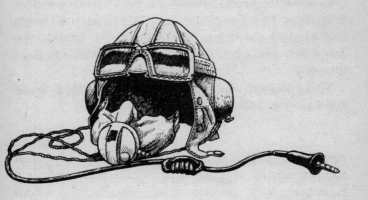

8

You are barely yards away from the edge of the forest when you feel the searing pain of a bullet in your back. You crash to the ground face-down, and slip away into the blackness of death.

Your adventure ends here.

9

The crushing weight of the earth above you slowly squeezes the breath from your lungs. Behind you, you can hear the desperate scrabbling of someone either trying to get out or attempting to save you. But it is too late anyway. The air is all but gone and you haven't the strength to draw another lungful. You will suffocate, here in the grave that you have literally dug for yourself.

Your adventure ends here.

10

The Group Captain shakes his head. 'You've not been here long, Thompson,' he says. 'We've thought about that route before, but it's too risky. I suggest you settle in a while before going off on any hair-brained schemes.'

Disappointed, you agree, salute and then leave. Now turn to **234**.

11

'Meet me at the Hotel Rochard in fifteen minutes,' says Madeleine, running off in the opposite direction from him.

The Germans follow you, but eventually you lose them in the winding streets. After walking a little longer, you double back and rejoin Madeleine at the Hotel as planned. Now go to **132**.

12

The plan is to cut the wire the night before the attempt, then mend it with fuse wire, so that when the escape attempt is made it can be done quickly.

You hear that the attempt is to be made soon, and desperately wish to take part in it. You must make a Persuasion skill roll to convince Dechant and the Escape Committee that you should be allowed to go. If you succeed, turn to **169**. If you fail, turn to **77**.

13

'We are . . . visiting our uncle here in Arras,' you reply.

'Ah yes, and where would he live?' the man replies.

'He . . . lives . . .' you stumble.

'He lives in a small village some five miles from here. He is a farmer,' Madeleine says, coming to the rescue.

'Very good, you may pass. Have a pleasant stay here,' he concludes.

Now go to **132**.

14

Instead of being taken back to your squadron for debriefing, you are driven to a quiet house in Hampstead.

Your driver has spent the whole journey telling you what has been going on whilst you were a prisoner, so you have no idea why you have been brought here. It is, therefore, with some trepidation that you get out of the car and walk up the steps of the house.

You are surprised to find a Major waiting for you.

'Welcome, Thompson, do come in. I expect you are rather exhausted after the last few days. I'm Major Dunbar by the way,' he says.

'Thank you, sir. I am rather tired, but I'm more curious. Why am I here?' you ask.

'Jackson will show you to your room so that you can change your clothes, then we'll talk,' is all the answer you get.

You follow Dunbar's batman up the stairs, and he shows you into a comfortable bedroom. There is a complete RAF uniform in your size laid out on the bed.

'If you need anything, sir, just ring,' Jackson says politely.

After a wash, shave and change of clothes, you feel at least half human again, and more than a little intrigued about the Major.

You go downstairs with an orderly, who ushers you into the lounge. The Major is talking to a naval captain. They both stop when they see you, and Dunbar gives you a drink while introducing you to Captain Greenwell.

'Do sit down, Thompson. I imagine you'd like an explanation,' he says.

You nod.

'How would you like to return to France?' he asks abruptly.

'I beg your pardon?' you say.

'Let me explain,' he goes on. 'You're one of the first to escape from Germany. We're looking for people with a recent knowledge of what's going on over there. We need to set up a network to carry out

27

sabotage, espionage, help organize the Maquis and get POWs out.'

'What are you, military intelligence?' you ask.

'Not quite,' he answers. 'We're the SOE, Special Operations Executive, responsible for covert action in Europe. How would you like to join us? We'd like you to work with the young French lady you brought back with you.'

Stunned, you take a moment to reply. Then you stand to attention and salute smartly. 'Sir, I would be honoured to be part of the SOE,' you say.

Your adventure ends here, for the time being at least.

Congratulations.

15

Releasing the handbrake, you press the accelerator to the floor. The vehicle lurches forward, its back wheels spinning on the gravel of the yard. The three Germans ahead turn and stare, then reach for their weapons. The gate out of the yard lies just ahead, but it is narrow. You must make a Driving skill roll. If you succeed, go to **199**. If you fail, turn to **130**.

16

You see a pair of Me109s tailing a Spitfire already hit and, diving almost vertically, you plunge after them. The rear German aircraft is just in your sights and hasn't seen you – a quick burst riddles his tail and he banks off to the right. Ignoring him, you follow the other down. Now turn to **79**.

17

All that now remains is to decide the date on which to

make the attempt, and indeed to thrash out how many of you will be taking the route. Go to **150**.

18

Stallard listens to your arguments and finally agrees that you should be one of the two to go. The attempt is to be made in two nights' time. In the intervening days, you must have a uniform made and passes forged. You visit the tailor and the forger and are delighted that the equipment provided is very good.

At last the evening of your departure arrives. You leave your hut already dressed in the uniform, and stroll across the compound with your Dutch colleague.

You walk up to the guard at the gate, and face your first test. You must talk to him. If your Language skill is greater than your companion's, make a Language skill roll. If not, use the Dutchman's Language skill:

Dutchman   Language skill 7

If either of you succeed, turn to **75**. If you fail, turn to **221**.

19

The corridor ends abruptly with only a ground floor window in front of you. However, it is large enough to climb through. Looking through it, you have a view of the yard at the back of the building. There is a truck parked in the yard and two German guards are standing smoking at the rear of it. Will you fire at the two Germans from the window (turn to **42**) or will you climb through and make a dash for the truck

– whose engine, you notice, is running – in the hope of driving it away (go to **251**)?

20

A court-martial is convened, presided over by Group Captain Evans, the S.B.O. This is your last chance to clear yourself. Make a Persuasion skill roll. If you succeed, turn to **292**. If you fail, turn to **106**.

21

You realize that there is no chance of success for you with Stallard's group, and decide to try something else. You can try tunnelling, if you have not done so already (go to **259**) or wire-cutting, again if you have not done so already (go to **191**). If you have tried both these options, turn to **257**.

22

The German is raising his rifle to shoot. You must make an Agility skill roll in order to get out of his line of fire. If you succeed, turn to **183**. If not, turn to **8**.

23

You start to run. For a moment, the searchlight loses you – enough time to get to the blind spot. Crouching down, you work feverishly at the wire. It takes time, though, precious time. Make a Luck roll. If you succeed, turn to **288**. If you fail, turn to **138**.

24

'I am French. You are RAF, no? I can help you get

out of Germany and perhaps to the Maquis, our resistance movement,' he explains.

Now go to **217**.

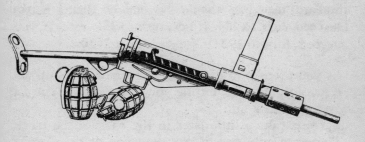

25

Early in the afternoon you visit the Belgian quarter-master who is in charge of the accumulated equipment stores for escapers. He has compasses, wire-cutters and even imitation weapons. Deciding what you will need takes up most of the rest of the day. Tomorrow, you may either go and see the forger in the morning (go to **162**) or the clothes makers in the afternoon (go to **68**). If you have already seen them both then go to **17**.

26

You move swiftly, but the guard fires instinctively and hits you. The searing pain of a bullet pierces your chest as you slip to the ground, mortally wounded.

Your adventure ends here.

27

For several days you help make false lids for the rubbish cans so that a man can climb in and out of them easily. The plan is to let three men escape in this manner. Make a Persuasion skill roll to convince Stallard that you should be one of them. If you succeed, turn to **184**. If not, turn to **21**.

28

As you prepare to kick him, the guard looks up and reacts instinctively, hitting you in the groin. You fall over and black out.

You awake a little later in the back of the truck. There are only five of you, and one of the German guards is rubbing a damaged shoulder.

'What happened?' you ask.

'We made a break for it after you got knocked out,' says Livermore, 'but they shot three of us and rounded up the rest. A bit of a shambles really.'

'Silence!' one of the Germans barks. They are obviously in no mood for anything now, and for safety's sake you decide to be quiet. Now turn to **47**.

29

Several minutes pass; then the guard returns and gestures for you to follow him outside. Now go to **179**.

30

The sky momentarily appears clear as you emerge from the clouds, still searching for the Me109. Ahead you can see the rest of your squadron and, banking around, you follow. Now turn to **36**.

31

The cooler is small and cramped and you find it difficult to live for days on end without talking to anyone. Luckily, during exercise period on the second day, you meet a veteran escaper, Peter Williams, who seems suitably impressed by your impromptu attempt. After a day or two of casual talk, he tells you that when you get out of solitary he will recommend you to the Escape Committee.

When you are released, Williams is as good as his word, and you find yourself co-opted on to the multi-national camp Escape Committee. Do you prefer tunnelling (go to **259**), wire-cutting (go to **191**) or working on methods to bluff your way through the main gates (go to **146**)?

32

It looks as though you have managed to convince him after reminding him of the Geneva Convention and its rules. You breathe a sigh of relief as he nods reluctantly.

'You may hear more of this later, when I have made further enquiries,' he says. Then he snaps orders to the guards behind you and they lead you from the room. Now turn to **177**.

33

You put your hands up and surrender. Two guards run out of the darkness and cart you off to the cooler. If this is your third visit, turn to **70**. Otherwise, turn to **31**.

34

You bob about in the dinghy for what seems like hours. The sky by now is empty and all you can see are the gulls circling above you. Darkness is closing in and you prepare yourself for a very uncomfortable night in the Channel.

As darkness descends, you hear the sound of a motor – not an aircraft, a ship! You tug at the bottom of your emergency flare and send a red rocket arcing into the sky, then sit back to wait.

Out of the darkness, a shape looms. It is a patrol boat. But as it comes closer and the searchlights mounted on its deck pick you out, you see to your horror that it is German, not English!

There is little you can do. You are about to become a prisoner of war. Now turn to **277**.

35

Looking around, you spot a long stout piece of wood and heft it determinedly. Half crouching, you hide behind a bush and wait for the approaching rider. As he roars up the road, you step out and immediately he brakes and tries to turn around. Like a flash you swipe at him, striking just below his helmet. The bike and rider skid across the road. He lies inert on the ground, and you quickly grab him by the feet and drag him into the bushes.

A thought crosses your mind: put on his uniform. No one will question a German despatch rider travelling along the country roads during the day. You don the grey-green tunic and trousers, buckle up the belt with its Mauser pistol in a holster, and finally place the slightly dented steel helmet on your head. Then you restart the Zundap and roar off westwards, triumphant. Now go to **131**.

36

The Germans are turning for home. Most of the bombers have dropped their loads in the sea – they won't hit London this time, you think.

'Red Leader here. Well done, gentlemen. Let's escort them home.'

'Roger,' you say into your R/T.

The scattered enemy are trailing off eastwards. Will you close with them (go to **200**) or will you keep your distance (go to **246**)?

37

You have no option but to surrender. Unceremoniously you are transported back to the camp, and brought to face the commandant.

'You have caused my men some considerable problems, but more importantly, you have made me look a fool,' he begins.

Not difficult, you think to yourself.

'The Luftwaffe cannot be held accountable for disruptive and reckless prisoners such as yourself, Thompson. I have no alternative but to hand you over to our own escape experts. Recently we have established a new camp, Oflag IV C, in a castle built by Augustus the Strong, King of Poland, and Elector of Saxony at the turn of the sixteenth century. It will become better known to you by the name your fellow prisoners have given it, Colditz. You will find the regime there a little less, well, gentleman-like. Good-bye Thompson, we will not meet again.'

Stunned, you salute, and resign yourself to the fact that you may not see England again until the war is over. Who can tell? What possibilities will present themselves, you wonder?

As you are escorted to the truck for transit to your new home, your mind turns over all sorts of ploys and ideas. Colditz will be a tough nut to crack. Your adventure in Stalag Luft 14 ends here . . . but who knows where it will really end?

38

He waves you away from the unconscious body of his comrade, then stoops to revive him. Now turn to 272.

39

Glancing to your left as you turn right, you spot a scout car pulling out of a side street. Keeping your foot on the floor, you gather speed. A lone German stands in the middle of the road in front of you and as you speed towards him he riddles the cab with gunfire. The burst hits you three times and, slumping over the steering wheel, you fight to avoid blacking out. Spinning the wheel and stamping on the brake, you slew the vehicle around and head back towards the gate and the scout car which is now moving towards you. Desperately, its crew try to stop you by emptying their guns into the cab, but to no avail. You are already dead as the truck hits the scout car and explodes.

Your adventure ends here.

40

Under questioning, it comes out that Parkinson is an Abwehr agent – a German. He was born in England and lived there most of his life, but was recruited early in 1935 by German agents. Since then he has been posing as an English officer, being placed in camps to inform on the escape activities of their occupants. It was only your memory of his one slip in conversation which unmasked him.

The sentence of the court martial is death for the spy. One night he is bundled out of his hut and thrown across the warning wire. The guards see nothing but a frightened man and shoot him without further investigation.

Your name has been cleared and you are free to return to your escape activities. If you have not tried escape with August Dechant, turn to **191**. If you have tried escape with him, but have not tried with John Stallard, then turn to **146**. If you have tried both then turn to **257**.

41

The damage is not too bad and your Spitfire is handling fairly well. Most of the Germans have turned around and are heading for home.

'Red Leader here. Well done, gentlemen. Let's escort them home.'

The scattered remnants of the German attack are being desperately defended by the Me109s – their pilots prepared to sacrifice themselves for their comrades. Will you close with them (go to **200**) or will you keep your distance, knowing your Spitfire is damaged (go to **246**)?

42

Make a Firearms skill roll. If you hit the first guard, try to hit the second with a second test of your skill. If you kill both, turn to **55**. If you miss either, they will fire back.

> First German guard   Rifle 6
> Second German guard   Rifle 7

Since you are firing from some cover, add 2 to their rolls when they try to hit you, reducing their chances.

If either of them are still alive after they have each fired two shots, turn to **64**. If you are hit and killed, your adventure ends here.

43

Livermore follows you cautiously as you cross the warning wire and make for the fence. He holds the wire as you cut it carefully and with as little noise as possible. You are almost finished when a searchlight passes very close. You duck and freeze, but it brushes over you. Test your Luck. If you succeed, turn to **268**. If you fail, turn to **96**.

44

You wait patiently for several weeks until another attempt is made. The first group has already passed successfully through the blind spot in the wire and it looks as if the Germans have been unable to find the break which has been carefully disguised with fuse wire. It seems worthwhile making another attempt by the same route.

As the night approaches, the last preparations are made. Equipment is provided, along with civilian clothes and even a compass each.

Assembling in the nearest hut to the hole, you wait until night has fallen before prising open the window and slipping out. With you go two Frenchmen, a Dutchman, another Briton and a Belgian. Together, you dash across the compound to the wire and, you hope, freedom. Now turn to **227**.

45

The combination flips over and crashes. Both Germans are killed. You remount your motor-bike and, taking a detour around the roadblock, head off west again.

You have only covered a few more miles when your bike runs out of fuel. Looking at the tank you see that a bullet from the combination's machine-gun hit and holed it.

Hiding the bike in the bushes and taking off the uniform you head across country. Now go to **5**.

46

The following day, you make an appointment to see

the S.B.O., Group Captain Evans. Carefully and fully you explain your plan to him and describe the blind spot in the wire. He does not seem wholly convinced. You must make a Persuasion skill roll. If you succeed, turn to **80**. If you fail, turn to **10**.

47

The German mood of anger and increased caution does not change. Indeed, when you reach the next stop at a local jail to pick up two more prisoners, they handcuff you to the wooden slatted seats in the truck. It seems you will be seeing Eastern France and probably Germany after all. Now turn to **289**.

48

Your ill-timed leap sends you sprawling to the ground unconscious, as you hit the side of a box-car.

You lie inert for several minutes, but gradually your senses come back and you struggle to your feet. Glancing around, you see several armed German soldiers approaching.

Cursing, you realize that it would be foolish to try to run. You place your hands on your head and start walking towards them. Now turn to **37**.

49

The woodcutter indicates that you should sit down. He grabs a length of rope and ties you up. Wagging a discouraging finger at you, he leaves. You sit alone on the floor cursing your bad luck and wishing that you hadn't gone into the hut in the first place. A few minutes pass and then you hear several voices outside.

The door opens and the grinning face of a German soldier appears. Now go to **37**.

50

Stallard's plan is to send two men through the front gate disguised as Goons. He is thinking carefully about who to send. Naturally, you want to be one of the pair. Make a Persuasion skill roll. If you succeed, turn to **18**. If not, turn to **173**.

51

The German does not return and, after a couple of hours, the train pulls into Paris.

The tannoy blares out German martial music, interspersed with virtually incomprehensible train announcements. Madeleine, however, knows where to go, and you walk swiftly to platform 16.

Luckily, the train is already waiting on the platform. You show the tickets and get on, this time picking a small carriage with just two rows of seats. No one else joins you in the carriage. After a few minutes the train pulls out.

'It will take about two hours or a little more,' says Madeleine. 'Why don't you get some sleep?'

'No, you sleep, I'll stay awake for a while,' you answer.

She does not argue, and is soon slumbering peacefully. You have not eaten for quite a while and you thrust your hand into your coat pocket hoping to find some food. Sure enough, Pierre has put an apple and some cheese in a bag.

As you begin your feast, you discover a letter with your name on it. Tearing it open you read:

43

Dear Flight Officer,

I had no opportunity to ask you personally, so I'm afraid that this letter will have to do, and it will leave you with little choice.

I fear my daughter, Madeleine, will be in grave danger if she remains here in France. As I told you the Germans are on to me. If they arrest me there is little chance that Madeleine will escape their notice.

Please try to get her safely to England. You are my only hope. I know that you will think her a burden, but she is quite capable of taking care of herself I assure you.

I apologize for doing this to you, but I have no other choice. After all, if you were in my position would you not do the same?

Thank you and good luck,
Pierre Blanchard

You stare at the letter for a long time before folding it up and putting it away. You decide to do as Pierre has begged you, but think it would be better not to tell Madeleine, she would only want to return to her father. You resolve to get her out of France, whatever problems your decision may bring.

The train is about to pull into Arras, so you gently wake her up. Now go to **129**.

52

As you get half-way across the road you are startled by the headlights of a truck. For a split second you are transfixed, then you begin to run. The driver has seen you, and screeches to a halt. Three armed soldiers leap out and give chase. Will you surrender (go to **37**) or will you run for it (go to **141**)?

53

A German sentry standing inside the wire, has spotted

you. He raises the alarm, shouting as he runs toward you, unslinging his rifle.

Will you surrender (go to **220**) or will you make a dash for the forest, about a hundred yards away (go to **22**)?

54

'Accidentally', you knock off the Goon's cap. Instantly, all the other prisoners cluster around to sympathize with him and ask him if he is all right. In the confusion, you scoop up the cap and pocket it. Walking rapidly away, you enter the latrines and press the cap badge into some soft wax so as to get an imprint of its design. Then you go quickly back to the crowd around the confused guard, dropping the cap among their shuffling feet. Another prisoner 'finds' it, and courteously returns it to its owner. Then you all move off and continue with your PT. Now turn to **50**.

55

Only seconds have passed, but both Germans lie dead. Suddenly you hear the sound of a rifle being cocked and then, 'Hände Hoch!' from behind you.

Dropping your weapon, you turn and see a scared soldier facing you with a machine-gun held in his unsteady hands.

The HQ is in turmoil. Germans appear from every direction; a red-faced officer strides up to you and snaps, 'For this you will be shot, Britischer!'

You are frog-marched to the commander's office. He is furious that people have been killed, and even more angry that it has happened within the confines of his headquarters.

'You are guilty of sabotage and murder, Englishman,' he says.

'It is the duty of every British officer to attempt to escape, sir. I regret the necessity of killing your men, but this is war,' you reply staunchly.

He seems determined to have you courtmartialled and shot. You must make a Persuasion skill roll to convince him. If you succeed, turn to **32**. If you do not, turn to **161**.

56

By the time you reach the outskirts of the village it is well past dawn. You feel very conspicuous, walking along in your RAF uniform. Hiding behind a wall you take off your jacket and tie and roll them up into a bundle, hoping that no one will notice the distinctive blue of your trousers.

One problem out of the way, your thoughts turn to your stomach. You are starving and, throwing caution to the wind, you go into a café just inside the village which sports the Tricolor, the flag of France.

You take the table furthest from the door and huddle for security behind the menu. An old couple eating breakfast look at you and then return to their meal. Presently a waiter appears and you stare meaningfully at the menu in front of you.

Will you point at what you want (go to **239**) or will you risk asking (go to **84**)?

57

The others agree that you should be in charge of the

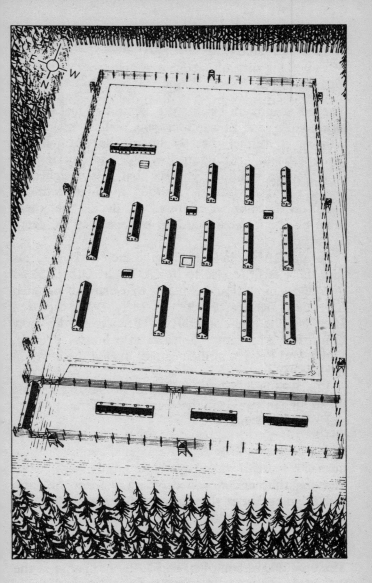

47

attempt and the decision as to when to go falls to you. You decide to leave in two days' time. Now turn to **227**.

58

The hut stands on brick stilts, some two feet off the ground. A wise precaution, you realize, making it difficult to tunnel directly under the hut without being noticed. Trotting up the steps and entering the long wooden building, you see that it is designed to house twenty prisoners. Making a rough estimate based on the number of huts, you decide that there must be about three hundred prisoners in the camp as a whole.

Several RAF men lie reading on their beds; it seems that there is little else to do. A Flight Officer Read introduces himself and explains that many of the men have been here since 1939 or early 1940, captured after landing their aircraft in France or the Low Countries. The camp, he says, also houses French, Dutch and Belgian airmen caught during the invasion of their countries.

You begin to feel tired, and after chatting a while about the progress of the war, nod off into a deep sleep. Now go to **176**.

(Illustration on previous page)

59

Revving the engine, you drive away from the gate, but a bullet passes through the thin wall of the cab behind you and shatters the windscreen. You wrench at the wheel in panic and the van turns off the road and drives straight into a drainage ditch. In seconds, guards from the gate surround you.

For this escapade you will get sixty days in solitary. If this is your third visit, turn to **70**. Otherwise, when you are released, you must decide what to do next. If you have not already worked with Moseby on tunnels, turn to **259**. If you have worked with him, but not with Dechant on wire-cutting, turn to **191**. If you have done both, turn to **257**.

60

Three Dorniers fly in a tight group just below you. Make a Pilot skill roll. If you succeed, turn to **123**. If you fail, turn to **175**.

61

Georges wakes you at 5.00 A.M., bringing with him a set of civilian clothes. He urges you to put them on quickly and come downstairs for something to eat. You wolf down a fine breakfast and then get into the truck.

'My plan,' Georges begins, 'is to pretend that you are asleep and use my brother's identity pass. The guards know him and are sure not to ask questions.'

'Where is your brother?' you ask.

'He is in northern Germany somewhere,' he replies. 'We do not see eye to eye about the running of the business, Henri and I, so he prefers the companionship of another French family who run a restaurant in Hamburg.'

Now go to **276**.

62

Thoughtfully you stroll around the wire, taking care to keep on the safe side of the thin strand of warning

49

wire which is about ten metres from the actual fencing. If you step over it you may be shot, at the very least you would spend a week in the cooler – solitary confinement – for the mistake.

Taking a second circuit, you notice that there appears to be a blind spot in the camp's defences. Along the perimeter, at a point nearest the coal store, it looks as though the nearest tower guard would not be able to see you if you got close to the wire. Will you come back after dark to test your theory? If so, go to **278**. If you would prefer to look for a different way to escape, go to **240**.

63

The sky is thick with aircraft: bombers, fighters, British and German. Many of the aircraft trail plumes of black smoke as they head for their final resting places in the Channel, and the sky is littered with the white blossoms of parachutes floating downwards. Your squadron is badly outnumbered and as two Focke Wulf fighters climb towards you, you have seconds in which to react. Make a Pilot skill roll. If you succeed, turn to **73**. If you fail, turn to **178**.

64

From the other side of the yard someone has managed to set up a machine-gun and is peppering the building with heavy fire. Ducking into cover, you consider your options. Will you surrender (turn to **72**) or will you continue to fight (turn to **250**)?

65

You make your calculated leap, but instead of hitting

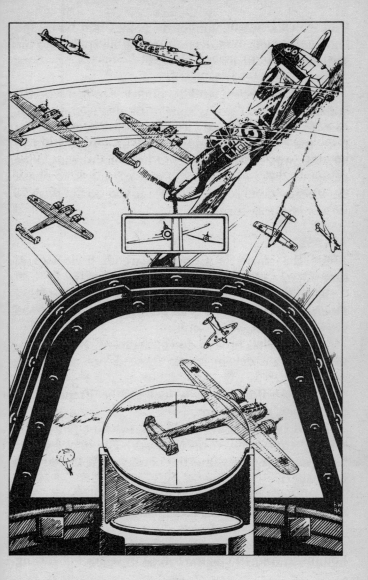

his cap, your outswinging arm catches him under the chin and knocks him over. Instantly he springs to his feet and draws his pistol.

'Cooler, Raus!' he bellows.

You are given a week's solitary confinement for your insolence. If this is your third visit to the cooler, turn to **70**. Otherwise, when you are released you have the choice of rejoining Stallard's group (go to **50**), working on tunnels if you have not already done so (go to **259**) or working on wire-cutting if you have not already done so (go to **191**). If you do not wish to do any of these, turn to **257**.

66

While the squad of Germans stretch their legs, a sergeant and two privates investigate your truck.

'What are you doing here at this time of night? Don't you know that it is an offence to be on the road after curfew?' says the sergeant.

'My truck has broken down, Sergeant. It is impossible to obtain decent spares these days,' replies the driver.

'I see. Hoffman, take a look at the Frenchman's truck,' says the sergeant.

The driver quickly wraps his machine-gun in an oily rag and throws it into the cab. The driver of the German truck peers into the bonnet with the air of a real expert.

'Ah, these damn French engines are useless. They can't take the pace, can they?' he remarks.

'No,' replies your driver.

The German fiddles about with a spanner for a few minutes and finally appears to be satisfied.

'There, try it now,' he says.

The engine starts first time.

'Merci, M'sieur. Perhaps I could give you this bottle of cognac for your trouble,' says the driver.

'Thank you,' he replies, hiding it under his tunic.

'You must return home now. We will say no more of this under the circumstances. Good night,' says the sergeant.

The Germans climb back into their truck and roar off in the opposite direction from Hesdin. You let them get out of sight and then continue your journey to the pick-up site. Now go to 71

67

You manage to knock the rifle out of the way and hit him squarely on the jaw. He falls unconscious and, grabbing the rifle, you rush out of the cell. Will you turn right (go to 286) or left (go to 245)?

68

The English outfitter used to work in the rag trade before he joined up in 1939 and he shows you a remarkable range of civilian clothes, all made from RAF and other uniforms, blankets and towels. Satisfied after having been measured, you thank him and leave. If you have not seen the forger, go to 162. If you have not seen the equipment supplier, go to 25. If you have seen them both, go to 17.

69

Banking tightly, you come around for a second pass. The three Dorniers have split up and are heading for home. It looks as though they have ditched their bombs in the sea, because they are moving faster now. Thumbing the trigger, you rake the fuselage of the stricken bomber – a shudder seems to run through the plane before it explodes in front of you. Make a Luck roll. If you succeed, turn to **213**. If not, turn to **247**.

70

Your persistence has drawn attention to you. The camp commandant will not put up with such disruptive and habitually awkward prisoners as yourself. He requests that you be transferred immediately upon your release from solitary and this is indeed what happens. Your destination? Oflag VIIC – Colditz!

Your adventure in Stalag Luft 14 ends here . . . but who knows where it will really end?

71

The pick-up site is a large open field two or three hundred yards off the main road. The resistance workers light small signal fires, then take up defensive positions around the landing field as a precaution.

Minutes seem like hours until eventually you hear the dull throbbing of an engine overhead. The plane circles once, then begins its approach for landing. Now is the moment when you must tell Madeleine that she is coming with you.

She is standing by the truck, watching the aircraft glide down to land.

'Madeleine, you must come with me to England. Your father made me promise to get you out of France,' you begin.

'No, I am needed here. I must return to my father for our work here has only just begun,' she replies.

Ebonar joins you and helps you to convince her.

Reluctantly, she finally agrees to come with you. The aircraft has now landed and the pilot is desperate to take off quickly. You cannot waste any more time.

Bidding farewell to Ebonar and the others, you both climb into the Lysander. Next stop England.

The flight is rather boring – cloud cover is low so there is little activity in the air. An hour and a half later, you land at an RAF fighter base in the south. A car is waiting to take you to London and another will take Madeleine to the Free French army headquarters.

After many days together you must now part. You give Madeleine your home address, and make her promise to write to you. Now go to **14**.

72

You throw your weapon to the ground and raise your hands. Two Germans run over to you and one kicks the gun out of reach as the other hits you across the face with the butt of his rifle.

'Schweinhund!' he screams as you fall to the gravel.

They drag you semi-conscious to the truck and, as you are thrown inside, you see that it is half full with other British prisoners. Still dazed, you introduce yourself.

Five of the prisoners are the survivors of a Blenheim crew: Flight Lieutenant Livermore, Flight Sergeant Johnson and their crew members McDonald, Robinson and Common. There are two others, fighter pilots like yourself: Parkinson and Cowie.

Before long the truck is ready to depart. Three

Germans sit in the cab and a further two join you in the rear. Both are young and nervous, one carries a machine-gun and the other a rifle. Cautiously, you look them over, then cast a meaningful glance at your fellow prisoners. It seems best that you wait until you are out of the town before trying anything. Now turn to **92**.

73

The leading Focke Wulf is a sitting target. A quick burst from your cannon sends it spinning out of sight. In a flash, the second aircraft fires, ripping through your right wing. The Spitfire shudders and the tip of the wing falls away. Realizing that you must bail out, you rip back the canopy. Make a Luck roll. If you succeed, turn to **280**. If you fail, turn to **74**.

74

Your foot is caught and you are trapped. The Spitfire is gathering speed as it falls from the sky. The cockpit is ablaze and there is no escape.

Your adventure ends here.

75

'Auf Wiedersehen,' he says as he lets you through.

'Guten Abend,' you reply. He closes the gate behind you and you walk briskly to the second, outer gate.

This time the guard inspects your passes, but then opens up and waves you through without comment. Holding back the smiles of relief, you continue your leisurely pace along the road and out of sight. Once around a bend in the road, you run into the forest and bury your mock uniforms. Shaking hands with your fellow escaper, you split up. Which way will you go? North-west towards Belgium (turn to **152**) or south-west towards Switzerland (turn to **139**)?

76

Make a Luck roll. If you succeed, turn to **67**. If you fail, turn to **26**.

77

They say no to your request. There are many others in the camp who have been here longer than you. You can of course go on the next attempt, but can you wait? If you wish to stay with Dechant's group and wait to make another attempt through the wire, go to **44**. If you do not want to stay with this group and have not already tried escape by tunnel, then turn to **259**. Or if that does not attract you and you have not already worked with John Stallard, then turn to **146**. If you have tried all of these, then turn to **257**.

78

You hear a gunshot, then a scrabbling sound at your window. Leaping out of bed, you see the scared face of a man dressed in civilian clothes. He is banging on the window. Opening it quickly, you stand back as he climbs in. Now turn to **157**.

79

The second Me109 is moving fast, twisting back and forth in an attempt to stay on the tail of the stricken Spitfire.

'Stay calm, Roy,' you tell your fellow pilot.

'Controls are smashed to hell. Hurry up, Alistair,' he shouts.

The Me109 has seen you now and pulls away from the plummetting Spitfire. You follow it. Make a Pilot skill roll. If you succeed, go to **231**. If you fail, go to **201**.

80

You succeed in persuading him, and he suggests that you wait until tonight, when he will arrange an emergency Escape Committee meeting.

The rest of the day passes slowly, and after evening lock-up you wait impatiently in your bunk until, at about 11.00 P.M., an unknown Dutchman appears in your hut and asks you to follow him. Doing so, you leave the hut by a side window and are then taken across the camp to the French section.

One of the huts has been taken over by a large group of senior officers. You salute as you enter and introduce yourself. Recounting your conversation with Group Captain Evans – who supports your idea – you explain your plan. You must make a further Persuasion skill roll to convince them totally. If you succeed, turn to **94**. If not, turn to **172**.

81

Make a Luck roll. If you succeed, turn to **290**. If you fail, turn to **291**.

82

In a matter of minutes the Germans have lost nearly forty aircraft. You cannot make a guess as to your own side's losses. However, there are still plenty of targets and the Germans are not calling it a day yet.

'Bandit on your tail, Alistair!' you hear over the R/T chatter.

Instinctively you glance back, but see nothing. Make a Pilot skill roll. If you succeed, turn to **203**. If not, turn to **143**.

83

When you awake the train is stationary. From both ends of the train you can hear German voices. Poking your head out of the box-car, you see that they are searching the train. You have no idea where you are.

You must make a run for it. Unfortunately, as you step from the train a shout tells you that they have spotted you. What will you do? Run for it (go to **141**) or surrender (go to **37**)?

84

Make a Language skill roll. If you succeed, turn to **239**. If you fail, turn to **109**.

85

They are not at all satisfied with your explanations or your ability to speak the native tongue. From the direction of the hut, a cry goes up. The soldiers look at you. You have no choice but to run. Now go to **141**.

86

You awake as the boat pulls into Calais harbour. The scars of the bitter struggle for this town only a few months ago are still obvious. The docks are littered

with half-submerged ships, blocking channels and denying the Germans the full use of the harbour.

The wharves are alive with activity. Dock workers are busy unloading cargo while German soldiers stand guard in impassive ranks and staff cars roar up and down the quayside.

Presently, the boat's crew throw lines to the shore and soon the boat is tied up. Boxes of ammunition and stores are strewn carelessly about. What you would give for a bomber squadron attack here!

The E-boat captain gestures for you to rise and reluctantly you drag yourself to your feet. Following the captain, you jump off the boat and head into the crowd. Close behind you follows a second member of the crew. Now turn to **295**.

87

As you poise to snatch the rifle, he looks up. Will you kick him (turn to **113**) or, realizing the odds against you are too high, will you forget the escape attempt (turn to **95**)?

88

The burst of fire catches you as you are about to make a dash for it. Several bullets find a home in your chest and the forest fades into darkness as you slump to the ground.

Your adventure ends here.

89

In the distance you can hear dogs barking; they must have picked up your trail. The countryside offers you little cover, and back along the road towards the east you can hear the roar of a motor-bike. Will you continue west (go to **171**) or will you try to ambush the bike as it passes (go to **35**)?

90

Painstakingly, you edge your way past the barbs in the wire and make a dash across open ground towards the cover of the trees which surround the camp. All the searchlights are pointing inwards, and darkness hides you until you reach the woods. Slowing, you pause to regain breath and composure, then look around you. Which way will you go? South-west, towards Switzerland (go to **139**) or north-west, towards Belgium (go to **152**)?

91

You reach the edge of the forest and find yourself by a road. Stopping for a moment, you hear the sound of an engine not far off but, more frightening, is the barking of the guard-dogs which seems to be drawing closer. Will you head off further into the forest (go to **242**) or will you cross the road (go to **102**)?

92

The truck follows the road to Lille. Every mile is clogged with German equipment heading for the coast. You seem to be the only ones going inland. Presently, the lorry stops at the side of the road in a small wood and the two guards jump out before gesturing to you all to follow them and stretch your legs. This could be your opportunity to escape. Will you try to wander off on your own (go to **235**) or will you stay with the main group and see what they decide to do (go to 3)?

93

Half crouching, you must make up your mind which way to go. As you rise, another burst of gunfire rips through the bushes close by. Make a Luck roll. If you succeed, turn to 229. If you fail, turn to 88.

94

They seem to be impressed with your idea – simple but effective, they think. After some discussion, they decide to co-opt you on to the Escape Committee and offer you the services of their specialist departments.

Thanking them, you leave in the same manner as you arrived. In the morning, one of the Dutchmen you saw the night before takes you aside to tell you what is available. Will you visit the forgers' hut (go to 162), the equipment-making and suppliers for food and compasses (go to 25) or will you see what the tailors can do to fit you out with civilian clothes (go to 68)?

95

Livermore is talking earnestly to Johnson. Suddenly, as you watch, they begin fighting. The two guards move quickly towards them to stop the fight. As they approach the struggling pair, the other five men rush them. After a flurry of blows and echoing gunshots, the scene clears to reveal three RAF men lying inert on the ground and one of the guards rubbing a bruised arm. Both Germans are extremely angry and one screams at you to rejoin the group. Moving carefully in order not to alarm them, you do as they wish. The three other Germans emerge hurriedly from the undergrowth and help to drag the bodies away. The remaining six of you are herded aboard the truck. Now go to **47**.

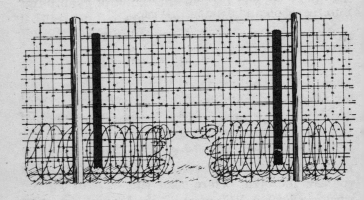

96

You have been spotted. Will you surrender (go to **33**) or will you run for it (go to **124**)?

97

Most of the parts of a German uniform can be faked without too much trouble, but one of the hardest things to fake is the cap badge worn by all the guards. Stallard gives you the difficult job of obtaining one that they can copy.

After thinking it over, you decide that the best way is to 'accidentally' knock off a Goon's cap. You describe your plan to several willing helpers and then select your victim, a particularly dumb-looking guard.

In company with several other prisoners, you pretend to be doing PT exercises, working your way towards your target. As you get close to him, your routine moves into 'squat' jumps, which involve squatting on your heels, then jumping into the air quickly, over and over again. The plan is to knock into the Goon and dislodge his cap.

Now test your Agility skill. If you succeed, turn to **54**. If you fail, turn to **65**.

98

As you squeeze through the gap, your tunic sleeve catches on a barb. The more you struggle, the worse it gets. Make an Agility skill roll. If you succeed, turn to **90**. If you fail, turn to **138**.

99

The railway sidings are on the outskirts of Metz. Keeping to the bottom of the ditch by the track you soon find yourself in the countryside once more.

You are miles from the camp; Luxembourg lies some thirty miles to the north, and Paris is now just one hundred and fifty miles away. The coast you reckon to be still a mammoth two hundred miles or so off to the north-west. Now go to **284**.

100

The driver is nowhere to be seen – a piece of luck. Make a Driving skill roll. If you succeed, turn to **211**. If you fail, turn to **59**.

101

Sickeningly, Madeleine was one of the casualties. Her

body lies slumped over a tree trunk far off to your left. She had come so far with you, and for her to be killed within a mile of safety makes you blame yourself for firing the first shot.

There is nothing you can do. The remaining resistance workers take care of the bodies and collect up the weapons. The pick-up is due in fifteen minutes. Ebonar takes your arm and bundles you into the cab of the truck and you speed off towards the landing site.

Ebonar lights a number of small fires, and together you wait patiently for the approach of the Lysander. Feeling very conspicuous, you seem to wait for ever, illuminated by fires in the middle of a meadow. The Germans would have a field day if they came along now.

Presently, you hear the drone of an aircraft engine close by. At last the plane has arrived. The pilot makes a flawless landing in the field. Embracing Ebonar you climb into the plane, and it taxis off, next stop England.

The flight is uneventful, there is low cloud in the area, so aircraft operations are limited. You land an hour and a half later in southern England. You thank the pilot and get into the waiting car.

Now go to **192**.

102

Just as you put a foot on to the road a headlight appears out of the darkness. It is moving very quickly your way.

Will you dash across the road (go to **209**) or will you dive for cover (go to **187**)?

103

You are waved through after a brief conversation. The sergeant believed your story of having to ride to Strasbourg to deliver a personal letter from your commanding officer to his mistress. The sergeant even gave you a chit to draw petrol from the depot at Strasbourg for your return journey.

Without looking back, you make all speed south. By nightfall you reach Mulhouse, just short of the Swiss frontier. Basel is about ten miles away. You drive to the border on your last drop of fuel.

You dump the bike and uniform in a ditch and consider a way to cross the border itself. Since you are in France the border defences are minimal. You can detect little in the way of German patrols in the area. Cautiously you cross the no-mans-land towards Switzerland and freedom.

After a mile or so you are challenged by a uniformed man. You still have your German pistol. Will you shoot (go to 117) or will you try to communicate? If so, make a Language skill roll. If you succeed, go to 266. If you fail go to 154.

104

The door is not locked. It opens inwards and, peering around the edge, you see four German soldiers sitting at a table playing cards. They have not yet heard you and seem engrossed in their game. Will you enter the room and attempt to capture them (go to 168) or will you shut the door softly and continue along the corridor, hoping to find a way out of the building (go to 19)?

(illustration on following page)

105

As you struggle through the undergrowth you hear a twig snap off to your left just before a commanding voice says, 'Hande Hoch!'

Even elementary German lets you understand 'Hands Up', and without much of a choice, you do so. A burly German sergeant emerges from a thicket with a submachine-gun and, pointing first at you then back in the direction you have come, makes it clear that you should return to the truck. You have no doubt he will be following closely behind. Now turn to 255.

106

Nothing that you can think of to say has any effect on them. They are wholly convinced of your guilt. With desperate thoughts racing through your mind, you hear the court pronounce its sentence – the sentence of death. Under the circumstances, they will arrange for this to be at the hands of the Germans.

You are confined to your hut, and the others in the building keep close watch on you. After night has fallen, several men appear at your bedside and cover your head. They bundle you outside and push you along silently. Then, suddenly, the cover is removed and your captors disappear into the night.

Staggering a few steps forward, you trip and fall over the warning wire. Before you can decide on a course of action, sirens wail loudly in your ears and a searchlight pins you like a fly to the ground. Almost as one, several shots ring out. Death comes mercifully quickly.

Your adventure ends here, ignominiously.

107

You swerve around and head back the way you came. Immediately you hear the sound of another motor-bike starting up. Going as fast as you can, you speed along the winding country road but, try as you may, the other engine gets louder all the time.

Bringing your machine to a halt, you decide to lie in wait and shoot it out with your pursuer. The approaching vehicle is a motor-cycle combination, with one man driving and the other in a side-car with a machine-gun mounted on the front. As they come around the corner, they see you. You both fire together.

Motor-cycle crewman   Machine-gun 8

As they are travelling fast, add 1 to each of your and their dice rolls, making it slightly harder to hit.

If you hit, and they do not, go to 45. If you are hit go to 141.

108

Two of the patrol nod to you as they pass and head towards the hut, the remaining five stop you. Make a Language skill roll. If you succeed, go to 111. If you fail, go to 85.

109

You stumble over your words, then swear in English. The man looks startled. He leans over you and whispers, 'Are you English?'

Will you reply, 'Yes,' (go to 258) or will you deny it (go to 24)?

110

Coming out of your dive towards the fighters, a lone Me109 glides gracefully past you at over 350mph. Banking around, you attempt to follow.

Make a Pilot skill roll. If you succeed, turn to **137**. If you fail, turn to **222**.

111

The men seem convinced that you are indeed a woodcutter, despite the fact that they have never seen you in the area before. You wave farewell and quicken your step until you reach a main road. Now go to **7**.

112

Your burst cuts down your prisoners and hits one of the two other Germans. But your magazine is now empty. The weapon belonging to the fallen guard lies on the ground and you dive towards it just as the remaining guard lifts his own weapon. Make a Luck roll. If you succeed, go to **147**. If you fail, he will shoot you before you can reach the weapon – in which case, your adventure ends here.

113

Make an Agility skill roll. If you succeed, go to **182**. If you fail, go to **28**.

114

The Me109's cannon burst hits the engine of your Spitfire. Thick oil and glycol cover your windscreen and tongues of flame lick menacingly towards the cockpit. You have no choice but to bail out. Ripping back the canopy, make a Luck roll. If you succeed, go to **280**. If you fail, go to **74**.

115

Your two most obvious choices are Livermore and Johnson. Whom will you choose? If it is Livermore, turn to **189**. If it is Johnson, turn to **118**.

116

You close the door quietly and run off south-west, eventually reaching a main road. Will you cross it and continue south-west (go to **7**) or will you follow it westwards (go to **281**)?

117

At this range you can barely miss. The soldier drops and you run towards him. To your horror you see that he was a Swiss border guard.

With despair you stoop over the body of the man. You have travelled so far, only to make a mistake like this.

Rising slowly you turn to leave, when suddenly a shot rings out. As you fall to the ground you can see a second Swiss soldier sprinting towards you. Your adventure ends here.

118

Johnson readily agrees to your plan and you decide to make your attempt that night.

You leave through the same window as before, and make your way across the compound. Suddenly, Johnson slips and falls over. Without thinking, he curses aloud. Instantly, a searchlight is swung towards you and the alarm goes off. The huts are too far behind for there to be any chance of regaining their safety. Will you stay here and surrender (go to **260**) or will you make a dash for it (go to **23**)?

119

Making wire-cutters could be a problem. Wisely, the Germans do not allow much metal in the compound. But as you pass the kitchen the following day, you catch sight of two long knives. Acting on impulse, you dash in through the open door, snatch the knives and conceal them beneath your tunic. Now go to **223**.

120

The truck stalls. Desperately, you try to restart it but have no success. German soldiers are heading towards you from every direction and you have no option but to surrender. Now go to **135**.

121

You keep to the edge of the forest for as long as you can. As the road begins to turn south-west, the forest

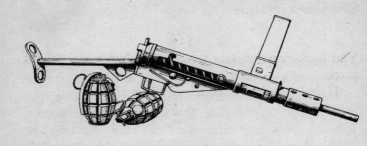

starts to thin out. Will you cross the road (go to **52**) or will you keep to the north of it (go to **89**)?

122

As you race down the steps of the station a burst of machine-gun fire rings out. Madeleine screams as she is hit. Stooping to pick her up, you realize that she is beyond help. Another burst narrowly misses you, spraying the wall with shots. You leap down the last few steps but a single shot from a pistol catches you in the leg, and a German marksman finishes you with another burst.

Your adventure ends here.

123

With your cannon button pulsing under your thumb and the whole aircraft trembling with the recoil of your Browning machine-guns, you see the middle Dornier lurch slightly and oily smoke begin to belch from its engine. Will you turn around for a second pass (go to **69**) or will you fly off in search of other prey (go to **36**)?

124

You have nearly reached freedom when a searchlight catches you.

'Halte!' you hear. Now turn to **33**.

125

You peer through one of the windows and see a man in civilian clothes running towards your hut. Reacting instinctively, you open the window and beckon urgently to him. He looks frantically around before veering towards you and vaulting head-first through the window. Now go to **157**.

126

'So you are going to Paris?' a heavily accented German voice enquires.

'Yes,' replies Madeleine, 'with my brother, Emile.'

'Your brother, eh? So he wouldn't mind if you went to the theatre with me at the weekend? We German officers always get the best seats for all the good shows, you know,' he continues.

'Well . . . I'm not sure that my husband would take too kindly to it,' she counters.

'And where is he?' asks the German.

'In Paris, waiting for me at the station, I hope,' she says desperately.

Will you continue pretending to be asleep (go to **297**) or will you help her get rid of the German (go to **279**)?

127

Feeling more relaxed, now that you know you can trust Georges, you fall asleep.

Abruptly you awake as he stops the truck and turns off the engine.

'Where are we?' you ask.

'In France,' he replies, adding with a smile, 'We crossed the border with no trouble, brother. This is where I must leave you, though,' he goes on. 'Cross the street to the house opposite and ask for Monsieur Pascal; tell him that I sent you, and that you are RAF. He will get you home somehow.'

'Thank you, Georges,' you say as you clasp his hand. 'Take care of yourself; I hope that we will meet again when the war is over.'

He nods and gestures for you to hurry. Now go to **165**.

128

Climbing into an open box-car and pulling the tarpaulin over you, you settle down for the free ride. Now go to **210**.

129

Taking Madeleine by the arm you get out of the carriage. Although the train is not full there is a considerable crowd on the platform. Gradually you ease your way through the throng and head for the ticket barrier. There are two railway officials and three soldiers there checking the passengers as they pass.

Casually you approach them, getting out your tickets and your false travel authorizations. As you hand

them to one of the railwaymen, a sixth man, dressed in civilian clothes, comes up and takes them from him.

'What is your business here in Arras?' he asks.

Make a Language skill roll. If you succeed, go to 155. If you fail, go to 263.

130

The truck smashes into a gatepost and judders to a halt. Leaping out of the cab, you see several Germans almost upon you. There is little you can do but surrender. Now turn to 72.

131

The motor-bike's tank is nearly full and you reckon that you could get about a hundred miles further south before you run out of petrol, providing you do not have to make any large detours. If all goes well, you should be able to get within fifty miles of the Swiss border.

Your journey takes you through the outskirts of Mainz, a major city, and then you make for Ludwigshafen. You are only ten miles from the town when you see that the road ahead is blocked.

Will you try to bluff it out (go to 185) or will you turn around and go another way (go to 107)?

132

You arrive safely at the contact address, knowing that your only hope is to get out of town quickly. The Germans must be on to you by now, in spite of the care you have taken. Your contact man, Monsieur Ebonar, welcomes you and hides you in his loft.

He has a crystal radio set and says that he will organize your next move with London. But he cannot afford to take risks, and only uses his radio at pre-arranged times and for short periods.

Finally he has some news for you:

'You will be picked up by Lysander in a field near Hesdin not far from here. We must be careful, the Germans know that you are in the area, and are still looking for you. Madeleine, my dear, you must return to your father, it is not safe for you to stay here any longer. M'sieur Thompson, you will leave for the pick-up point later tonight.'

'Could I speak to you for a moment . . . alone,' you ask.

'Of course,' he says. Then, turning to Madeleine, adds, 'Excuse us, my dear.'

Madeleine goes downstairs, and you wait until she is out of earshot.

'I have promised her father to get her out of France, she will have to come with me,' you tell him.

'Impossible . . . this is not possible,' he says firmly.

You show Ebonar the letter. He reads it carefully and reluctantly agrees with you.

'You are right,' he says, 'it would be best if she did leave France, so I will arrange for you both to get to Hesdin.'

Now go to **159**.

133

You rise to leave, furtively glancing around. The old couple have left and you are alone in the cafe. Slowly you head towards the door. All of a sudden the waiter reappears and shouts to you:

'Wait, please,' he calls in English.

Stunned, you stop and watch as he walks towards you. Now turn to **217**.

134

Georges tries to stop you as you leap from the truck. A volley of fire smashes the windscreen and the truck careers off the road, throwing you into the bushes. As your senses jar back into action, you hear the heavy footfalls of running men. Instinctively you head off into the undergrowth. Bullets whistle past as the soldiers catch sight of you, and you are sure they are gaining on you. Will you continue to run (go to **141**) or will you surrender (go to **37**)?

135

As you jump out of the truck, you see several armed Germans running towards you. Now turn to **72**.

136

As you reach the guard, he spins around and points his rifle at you, shouting, 'Halte!'

Will you rush him (go to **76**) or, certain that he will fire before you can reach him, will you give up the idea and sit down (go to **29**)?

137

Raking the fuselage of the Me109 from above, you see a spurt of flame leap out as it begins to plummet towards the ground far below. First kill of the day!

Now turn to **82**.

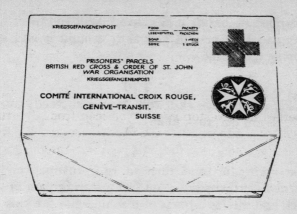

138

As you continue to struggle on the wire, you drop
your cutters and they strike a rock on the ground.
The sound seems to echo across the whole compound.
Almost at once, a searchlight departs from its random
track and moves steadily towards you. Soon, you are
in the centre of a pool of brilliant light. Seconds later,
you hear the chatter of a machine-gun. It is the last
sound you will ever hear – the guards have orders to
shoot on sight at night.

Your adventure ends here.

139

You head off into the forest, constantly turning to
make sure that no one has seen you. Gradually the
camp fades from view and, afraid of getting lost, you
try to decide in which direction you should be
travelling.

After maintaining a brisk pace for fifteen minutes
or so, you enter a clearing. A small wooden hut with

logs piled up beside it lies ahead. Will you investigate it (go to **170**) or will you skirt around it and keep moving (go to **186**)?

140

Make a Language skill roll. If you succeed, turn to **267**. If you fail, turn to **261**.

141

You spring up and turn to run. Instinctively the startled Germans fire. You feel a searing pain in your back and side as a burst of machine-gun fire rips into you.

Your adventure ends here.

142

You manage to creep up behind him successfully and deliver a blow to his neck. The guard slumps to the ground. Quickly, you pick up his rifle and rush out of the cell. The corridor goes left and right – which way will you turn? If you go left, turn to **245**. If you go right, turn to **286**.

143

You feel the Spitfire shake as an Me109 fires into your tail. Diving violently away to the left, you hope that someone is behind him.

The answer to your prayer comes quickly.

'Got him, Alistair! He's a flamer.'

'Thanks, Dick – took your time!' you answer with relief.

'That's gratitude! You owe me a drink,' says your comrade.

The Germans are turning for home now, their formation in tatters. Will you try to catch them up (go to **200**) or will you keep a respectful distance (go to **246**)?

144

The camp is alive with activity: football, open-air language classes and many men just walking around the perimeter. Everywhere there are RAF uniforms, mixed with those of other nationalities – French, Dutch and Belgian. It appears that roughly a third of the prisoners are French, a third British and the remainder a mixture of Dutch and Belgians. Many have been here since just after war broke out in 1939.

Feeling that you need a rest before you inspect the camp properly, you make your way to Hut 113 with Livermore and Johnson. As you enter, a Flight Officer by the name of Read introduces himself and shows you to your bunks. Taking the top bunk in a tier of two, you nod off into a deep sleep. Now go to **176**.

(illustration on previous page)

145

You are taken to one of the French huts and go inside. The Senior French officer and several others are sitting at a table, engaged in a game of cards. After you have been introduced to them, they agree that you should join the Escape Committee. There are three main ways of escaping from the camp: Under, Over and Through. That is, by tunnel, by cutting the wire or by bluffing your way past the guards at the front gate. Which do you prefer? If it is Under, turn to **259**. If Over, turn to **191**, or if you prefer Through, turn to **146**.

146

John Stallard is the man responsible for organizing diversions and bluffing his way past the guards. Most of his men are seasoned Goon-baiters and Scroungers and there is not much he cannot lay his hands on. He has two schemes going at the moment and offers you the choice of either one: working on a uniform bluff through the main gate (go to **97**) or helping organize an escape in the rubbish van which comes to the camp weekly (go to **27**).

147

You grab the dropped machine-gun and open fire, cutting down the remaining guard. Climbing to your feet, you gaze round the yard, searching for signs of any further trouble.

Suddenly, two Germans run from a building on the other side of the yard. Reacting without thinking, you swing the machine-gun and cut them down. Now turn to **55**.

148

Covering them with the machine-gun, you herd them into the corridor. Turning left, you pass your empty cell and the unconscious guard before you emerge into the yard. Two guards stand to the rear of a stationary truck, whilst three more loiter some yards from the front of the vehicle. Will you make your presence known (turn to **215**) or will you approach the truck as quietly as possible with your hostages (turn to **282**)?

149

Walking out into the compound, will you go straight to inspect the wire perimeter (go to **62**) or will you have a look around the huts first (go to **240**)?

150

You are introduced to August Dechant, the wire-cutter organizer. As soon as you outline your idea, he is enthusiastic and helpful, laying down the ground rules and introducing you to the rest of his team. Now go to **169**.

151

The sirens shatter the silence of the night as you hurriedly disappear into the forest. The guards have already set the dogs loose hoping to pick up your trail. For the moment, though, you still have the element of surprise. Sensing the need to make all speed, you head off north-west. Now go to **91**.

152

The forest is very dark, with little light penetrating the ceiling of branches and leaves above you. The going is treacherous; fallen branches litter the ground and the undergrowth is dense. After half an hour you finally reach the edge of the forest.

To the west you can see the lights of a village. Will you go there (go to **56**) or will you head for the train track which runs roughly north-south (go to **269**)?

153

Frantically, you begin to worm your way backwards.

It seems like hours rather than seconds before you feel hands tugging at your legs. The panicked scrabbling of your body turns presently into a smooth slide backwards, and you emerge, choking and spluttering, into the musty air of the remnants of the tunnel.

The tunnel has been set back by at least a week – maybe more. After your accident, you are given the less hazardous task of a 'Stoolie' – a lookout.

Several days later, you are on duty outside the storeroom, casually leaning up against the wall, when you see three guards purposefully striding towards you. What will you do? Create a diversion (go to 265) or rush into the storeroom and warn those below (go to 158)?

154

The man does not seem to understand you. Will you try again? If you succeed, go to 266. If you fail or do not wish to try again, turn around and disappear into the darkness. Then go to 5.

155

What will you tell him? That you are staying with relations, (go to 13) or that you are just passing through (go to 4).

156

Close-by you hear dogs barking. The German search parties are very near and you decide that if you are challenged you will try to bluff your way out.

From the bushes to your right an armed patrol breaks cover and heads towards you. Will you run for it (go to **141**) or will you continue to walk west, towards them (turn to **108**)?

157

The man is a Belgian and wearing very good imitation civilian clothes. He speaks little English, but is obviously grateful for your help. You manage to understand that his escape attempt went wrong when he nearly blundered into a dog-patrol several huts away. He panicked and ran, but does not think that anyone had actually seen him until a searchlight caught him in its beam for a second. He managed to evade it and is fairly sure that the Germans did not see him enter your hut by the window.

The following day, your visitor manages to merge with the other men in your hut as they leave for Appel and is able to rejoin his own comrades without being spotted. Later on in the morning he reappears and, with a big smile, he takes you to meet the camp Escape Committee. They seem suitably impressed by your quick thinking of the night before, and offer to co-opt you on to the committee. You may choose in which area you would like to work: tunnelling (go to **259**), escape over or through the wire (go to **191**) or methods of bluffing your way through the gates (go to **146**).

158

Rapidly, the three tunnellers emerge, covering the trapdoor in a flash. The three Germans enter and, despite your protests and attempts to divert them, walk straight up to the trapdoor and open it.

The four of you are arrested and each is given a

month in the cooler. The tunnel is filled in by the Germans. Now go to **233**.

159

When you next see Madeleine she tells you that Ebonar has asked her to accompany you to the pick-up site. You feign surprise and tell her you are pleased that you do not yet have to say goodbye.

At the appointed time Ebonar gives you and Madeleine a sten gun – a simple but effective machine-gun, often nick-named the 'grease-gun'. You have never used one before, but Madeleine says it's easy. The only thing you have to watch out for is that the gun pulls upwards and to the left when you fire it.

You both climb into the back of a small truck with three other resistance people and head off out of town for the short drive to Hesdin.

All goes well until you reach the banks of the river Canche. Then, just along the road ahead of you, you see a vehicle coming your way. It must be German, no one is allowed to travel legally at this time of night. There is little cover and your truck cannot possibly turn around in time so you will have to silence the occupants of the approaching car.

Your truck shudders to a halt by the roadside. The driver opens the bonnet, placing his 'grease-gun' out of sight and pretends to look at the engine. The rest of you take cover in the sparse bushes nearby.

Presently the German truck arrives and pulls up beside yours. The driver gets out and you hear the clatter of many feet as the 'passengers' the truck is carrying climb out – a full platoon of German infantry!

Will you open fire immediately (go to **300**) or will

you hold fire, hoping your driver will be able to think up a story that will satisfy them (go to **66**)?

160

The guard leaves. You finish your food and coffee. Then you wait. A couple of hours later he returns and gestures for you to rise and follow him. Now turn to **179**.

161

You try to remind him of the Geneva Convention, but he shakes his head.

'Sabotage does not come under the Geneva Convention,' he says. 'I have the power to order a summary execution, and that is what I shall do. We have no time for dangerous prisoners, solely interested in causing trouble.'

He snaps some orders to your guards, and they grab you and take you outside. A sergeant appears with a column of a dozen soldiers. He strides over and offers you a blindfold as you are led to stand against a wall. Shaking your head, you refuse it and stand rigid, waiting for the inevitable.

'Take aim . . . fire!' shouts the sergeant.

Your adventure ends here.

162

The head forger is an Englishman called Needham, a tall, rather athletic man who used to work in the print business before the war. He is well versed in the ways of forgery. He can supply you with an Auschweis (German transit pass), identification passes and even

train tickets. Sorting out what you need takes up most of the morning.

You can now go to see the equipment suppliers in the afternoon (go to **25**) or you can wait until tomorrow and see the clothes makers (go to **68**). If you have already seen them all, go to **17**.

163

The S.B.O. is a fairly tall man in his middle forties, bespectacled and with a vaguely aristocratic air. He welcomes you warmly and offers you a seat. His quarters are quite comfortable, if a little cramped. In a soft voice he asks your names, ranks and serial numbers, jotting them down in a ledger on his desk. He assigns you to Hut 113, in the south-east corner of the compound and suggests you get some sleep after your journey.

You stand again, salute and leave. Will you go directly to Hut 113 (turn to **58**) or will you have a look around first (turn to **144**)?

164

After securing them to their chairs, you leave the guard room and return to the corridor. Turning right out of the room, go to **19**.

165

A middle-aged man answers your urgent knocking. You repeat what you have been told to say. A worried look appears on his face as he ushers you inside. With a last glance behind you, you see that your companion has already left. Now go to **195**.

166

As you take a step forward a floor board creaks under your weight. Instantly the woodcutter leaps and makes a grab for his axe.

As he brandishes the lethal weapon you realize that you can do little but give yourself up. Now go to **49**.

167

Standing up, you shout, 'I surrender! Don't shoot!'

From the bushes below and to the right two Germans appear and gesture for you to join them. They look extremely angry and very nervous. You do as they wish and scramble down the hillside towards them.

The walk back to the clearing is made in silence, with one German walking ahead of you and the other following. They order you and your remaining colleagues into the truck. Now turn to **47**.

168

Making sure the safety catch on the rifle is released, you carefully enter the room.

'Hands up!' you command.

Staring at you in disbelief, the Germans raise their hands. Quickly swapping the rifle for a loaded machine-gun, you stand for a moment in thought. What are you going to do now? Tie them up and leave them (turn to **164**) or take them with you as hostages (turn to **148**)?

169

Six are going, including yourself. The rest of the

party consists of two Frenchmen, a Dutchman, a Belgian and another Briton. The plan is straightforward and timed to take place when the guards have been on duty for a couple of hours and so are less alert.

Will you decide to put yourself forward as the leader of the group? If so, you must make a Persuasion skill roll. If you succeed, turn to **57**. If you fail, or if you decide not to become the leader of the escape attempt, then turn to **230**.

170

Listening at the door you can hear only a low murmuring sound. Cautiously you enter the hut. The owner is sleeping deeply on a makeshift bed. Will you leave immediately (go to **116**) or will you try to steal some food without waking the slumbering man (go to **248**)?

171

If you keep going west you will reach either the Luxembourg or Belgian border, but you believe that they are at least one hundred miles away. At a reasonable pace it would take you perhaps a week. The sun will be up soon and you need to find somewhere to hide. The motor-bike has passed, so cautiously you cross the road and head across the field to the south-west.

Ahead is a farm. As you approach it you can see that the farmer has already begun milking his cows. Keeping out of sight you slip into one of his barns and hide yourself in the hayloft.

Now go to **193**.

172

'We are grateful to you for pointing out a weak spot in the camp's defences,' says a French officer to you via an interpreter. 'But there are men in this camp who have been here for over a year. There is a waiting list for escape routes like the one you have found. Being newly arrived, you will have to go to the bottom of the list, at least for a while.'

You feel slightly annoyed at what he says, but you can see the justice in it.

He continues, 'But the fact that you have been here such a short time and have already spotted an escape route is very impressive. If you are willing, we would like you to join the Escape Committee. There are three main ways of getting out of here: Under, Over or Through, we call them. Tunnelling, wire-cutting or bluff through the gates. Which would you prefer to work on?'

If you decide Under, then go to **259**. If Over, then go to **191**. If Through, then go to **146**.

173

Stallard listens to your arguments, then tells you that you can be the stand-by, which effectively means No. After all, you haven't been in the camp very long. You decide to transfer and work on Stallard's other plan, to sneak men out in the rubbish truck. Now turn to **27**.

174

The vehicle takes the corner easily and you see the harbour area ahead. Behind you, you hear shots and screams as the Germans run out of the HQ building.

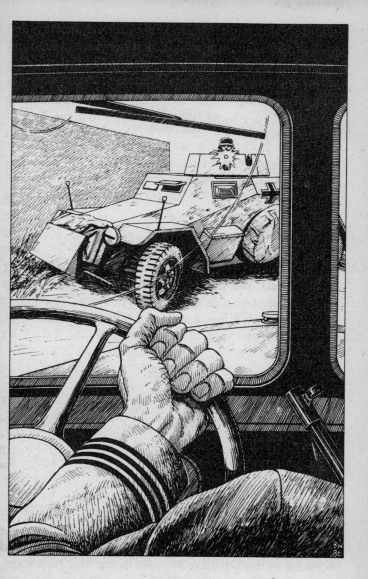

Two hundred yards up the road is a German scout car, and the crew have spotted you. The vehicle pulls across the road, blocking your way. Two soldiers run in front of the truck and raise their rifles, but you knock them down as you speed up the road. Impact with the scout car is imminent, though, and you grab your gun as you open the door, then jump.

The truck hits the scout car and explodes, showering pieces of scorched metal over the surrounding area. Staggering to your feet after the leap from the cab, you shoot at two Germans who are running towards you. Now turn to **55**.

175

The three aircraft provide a criss-cross of interlocking fire and you hear the thud of cannon shells ripping through your rear fuselage. Will you continue flying (go to **41**) or will you attempt to bail out immediately (go to **218**)?

176

You awake to the sound of a bell ringing. The officer on the bunk next to yours explains that it is the call to 'Appel' – daily parade and head-count. As you trot along to the assembly area at the rear of the camp, you discover that this happens at 8.30 A.M. and 4.00 P.M. every day. Apart from Appel and the ritual of locking the prisoners into their huts at 6.30 every evening, the Germans appear to leave the POWs to their own devices.

Arriving at the Appel area you see ranks of airmen, lined up by nationality, with their superior officers at the front. Most look sullen and despondent – hardly surprising when they have been here for so long.

The head-count is slow, with the 'Goons' (prison staff) running back and forth along the lines of prisoners. Presently you are all dismissed and rush off to line up for breakfast.

This is your first real opportunity to meet the rest of your fellow Britons. Will you bring up the question of escape (go to **237**) or will you start by asking for more details about the prison layout and routine (go to **236**)?

177

You are taken back to the cells and locked in. Now go to **29**.

178

The two aircraft zoom towards you and before you can act they have riddled your fuselage with cannon fire. The Spitfire shakes with the impact and great tongues of flame pour from your engine. Desperately, you rip back the canopy, knowing that you must bail out or fry. Make a Luck roll. If you succeed, go to **280**. If you fail, turn to **74**.

179

The yard at the rear of the Headquarters is deserted save for a truck with its engine running and two German soldiers standing sentry at the rear of the vehicle. Walking closer, you see that the truck is half full of British servicemen, all waiting to be driven to the POW camp. You climb aboard and introduce yourselves. It seems that the seven others in the truck were all picked up in the early hours of the morning from local jails.

Five of the prisoners are the surviving members of a Blenheim crew – Flight Lieutenant Livermore, Flight Sergeant Johnson and their flight crew, McDonald, Robinson and Common. The other two are fighter pilots like yourself – Parkinson and Cowie.

Before long the truck is ready to move off. Three Germans sit in the cab at the front and a further two join you in the rear. Both soldiers are young and nervous – one has a machine-gun, the other a rifle. Cautiously you study both of them, then look meaningfully at your companions. It seems best to wait until you are in the countryside before trying anything. Now turn to **92**.

180

You climb into a box-car of the train bound for Switzerland and settle down for the journey ahead. After half an hour or so, you hear a whistle to the rear of the train, then slowly the locomotive pulls away from the station. Gradually the rhythm of the train relaxes you and you fall asleep. Now go to **83**.

181

The woodcutter lies sleeping like a baby, oblivious of your presence. Will you knock him out (go to **225**) or will you kill him (go to **232**)?

182

Your kick sends the guard crashing to the gravel unconscious. His gun lies on the ground at your feet. The other German has spotted you by now, however,

and you must make a Luck roll. If you succeed, turn
to **38**. If you fail, turn to **274**.

183

Zig-zagging your way across the open ground, you
hear several shots but none come near you. You gain
the safety of the woods but, looking back, see that
two of your comrades have not been so lucky. Even
as you watch, a bullet grazes a tree stump only a few
feet from you. The others of your party have already
disappeared deeper into the woods. You are on your
own. Will you decide to head south-west towards
Switzerland (go to **243**) or north-west towards Belgium
(go to **151**)?

(illustration on previous page)

184

The rubbish will be collected in a few days' time.
The waiting is almost unbearable, but finally the time
passes and the day arrives.

The van drives into the camp at 9.00 A.M., and by
8.45 – just after Appel – you are safely hidden in a
rubbish bin. Crouching in the darkness, you hope
that whoever has the task of lifting the can on to the
van will not drop it!

You hear the sound of approaching feet and the
can in which you are hiding is lifted and carried for a
short time, then dumped with a clang into the back
of the van. You wait a little longer before hearing the
engine start and feeling the motion as the van drives
towards the main gate. The stench in the van is
disgusting and you feel a strong urge to cough. You
must make a Luck roll to restrain yourself. If you
succeed, turn to **212**. If not, turn to **194**.

185

You halt at the road block, and a Feldwebel, a German sergeant, approaches you. Make both a Persuasion skill and a Language skill roll. If you succeed with both, go to **103**. If you fail either or both of them go to **294**.

186

Ignoring the woodcutter's hut you continue to head vaguely south-west. Eventually you come to a main road which heads west and then south-west. Will you follow it (go to **281**) or will you cross the road (go to **7**)?

187

The motor-cycle combination stops near where you are hiding. One of the Germans seems to be insisting that he saw someone near the road. The other is not so certain. They both dismount and one turns the headlight towards the forest whilst the other moves towards you. Make a Luck roll. If you succeed, go to **241**. If you fail, go to **6**.

188

He offers you a seat, and is about to say something when the bell rings at the door.

'Customers,' he explains, 'you will excuse me for a moment.'

You nod, and he leaves the kitchen. Now turn to **228**.

189

Livermore is at first reluctant and wants to talk to

the Escape Committee about the attempt, but you
eventually persuade him that your plan is a good one
and that no one should know. You decide to make
the attempt as soon as possible. The next evening,
you open a window in your hut and you both slip out
and across the compound towards the wire. Now turn
to **43**.

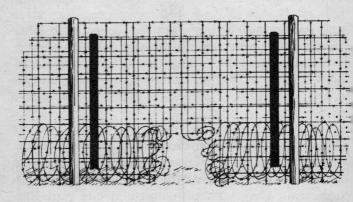

190

'My name is Georges Luboff, I am German by country
of birth, but French in heart: both my parents were
French. This was their business. I took it over when
my father died three years ago. My mother died some
years before. The Germans love my cooking, and I
am well known to them. I expect that we will have no
problems crossing the frontier, they trust me,' he
confides.

Georges takes you to the attic, where you find a
bed and little else. You nod your thanks to him and
he recommends that you sleep, it will be an early
start in the morning.

After he has gone you climb into bed. Do you trust him? If so go to sleep and wait for the morning (go to **61**). If you do not trust him, lie awake and wait for him to retire before making a break for it (go to **224**).

191

The wire specialist is a Belgian, August Dechant, who has only been in the camp about three months, but in that time he has been responsible for almost half the 'home-runs' – successful escapes – from the camp.

His English is impeccable and he has a multi-national team working for him. He outlines his current scheme and offers you a job working on it. Now turn to **12**.

192

The driver fills you in with what has been going on since you became a POW, and explains that he is taking you to see a Major Dunbar.

You arrive at a secluded house in Hampstead and the driver shows you to your room.

'Just ring if you need anything. The Major is waiting to meet you in the lounge downstairs,' he says.

You have a wash and shave, and put on the clean uniform lying on the bed. It fits perfectly, exactly your size!

Walking downstairs you knock on the door of the lounge. An orderly shows you in and introduces you to Major Dunbar and Captain Greenwell, the former an army officer, the latter a naval officer.

The major gives you a drink and asks you to sit down.

'I expect that you are wondering why you are here,' he begins.

'Yes sir, I am,' you reply.

'Well, we work for the Special Operations Executive, the SOE. We are responsible for covert actions against the Germans: sabotage, espionage, gun running, getting POWs back to England and helping the Maquis,' he explains.

'So what do you want from me?' you ask.

'We'd like you to join us, of course,' he replies.

Stunned by the honour, you take a moment to answer. Then you manage to rise to your feet and salute smartly. 'I would be proud to work with you,' you reply.

Your adventure ends here, but the war continues.

193

The day passes with you fitfully taking snatches of sleep, always aware that you could be discovered. No doubt the Germans are combing the countryside for you.

As darkness begins to shroud the buildings of the farm you must decide which way to go. Will you head back towards the road (turn to 281) or westwards across country (turn to 284)?

194

Unable to restrain yourself, you burst into a fit of coughing. Almost at once, there are shouts from outside the van.

'Achtung!' you hear, followed by a gunshot hitting a rubbish bin. Instantly, you leap to your feet with your hands in the air – and rubbish in your hair! It is the cooler for you, or is it? The van is stopped half in and half out of the main gate. Will you surrender (go to **296**) or will you try to make a break for it (go to **285**)?

195

'Welcome. My name is Pierre Blanchard, I own a chain of florist shops in this part of France. We have had several successes recently in getting escaped POWs back to England. I fear, though, that the Germans are on to us. It is too dangerous for you to stay here. I will send you to my friend in Arras, from there you are no more than a hundred miles from the coast,' he tells you.

'Thank you,' you reply. 'I appreciate the great risks you are taking in doing this. When will we leave?'

'In an hour hopefully. A train leaves for Paris at 4.30, you must change there and get on the train for Arras. The change-over is no more than five or ten minutes,' he continues.

'I am to go alone?' you reply in a concerned voice.

'Non, mon ami,' he says. 'I will have my daughter Madeleine go with you; she has escorted escapers before.'

He offers you a seat and you wait for him to make the last few arrangements. Half an hour later a young woman, no more than twenty years old, joins you in the room. She is wearing a brightly coloured dress and holds a trench coat over her arm.

'This is for you, M'sieur, I'm afraid we have little to offer you otherwise,' she says. 'We must leave now, my father will drive us to the station.'

You both join Pierre in his small Renault van and speed off towards the centre of town.

As you are about to get out, Pierre offers you a pistol. You look at it blankly at first, but he nods reassuringly. You take it, thank him and get out. Madeleine urges you to hurry and you walk together into the station.

'Stay close to me while I get the tickets,' she tells you.

You stand obediently next to her. In a few minutes, she has the tickets and you walk with her towards the platform. Now go to **197**.

196

Though the market is on the other side of the road, it offers you your best chance to evade capture. You are being pursued very closely and one of the soldiers fires a warning shot in the air, almost in desperation, as you disappear into the crowd.

The locals have no love for the Germans so they scatter to let you through; then bunch up and get in the way of your pursuers. Eventually you stop running, and head towards your contact address. Now go to **132**.

197

The train is almost deserted, few people think it wise to travel far in such bad times. The man on the platform gate punches your tickets and you walk a few carriages down the train before boarding.

After finding a seat, you still do not relax until you hear the guard's whistle and the train finally pulls away.

You manage to nod off to sleep, leaving Madeleine to look out for you. Presently you hear the faint murmurings of a conversation. Will you pretend to be asleep (go to **126**) or will you open your eyes (go to **279**)?

198

'67524 Flight Officer Alistair Thompson, sir!' you shout.

'You have nothing further to say?' he asks.

You stand silently at attention as he looks at you.

'I have no alternative but to hand you over to the Gestapo for interrogation,' he says finally. 'I am sorry.'

Realizing that you must speak quickly or else risk being handed over to the secret police, you recount your actions over the Channel. As you finish, he clears his throat and says:

'I am glad that you have chosen to cooperate, Thompson. I see no need for any further unpleasantness. You will be taken to Luftwaffe headquarters – they are responsible for downed RAF pilots. Goodbye.'

A Kubelwagon staff car is parked outside with three armed men in it and you are swiftly driven away to Luftwaffe HQ. Now turn to **256**.

199

The side of the truck grates against the gatepost, but it keeps moving. A broad road stretches right and left and you must make a quick decision. Will you go left (turn to **174**) or right (turn to **39**)?

200

The German bombers, even without their loads, are

much slower than you are and they weave right and left in an attempt to shake you off. Parachutes litter the sky as many crews abandon their aircraft and seek the comparative safety of the Channel. You are now about half way towards the French coast, closing at a speed of almost 400mph.

'Red Leader, Red Leader, new formation of bandits heading our way. Estimate fifty – all fighters!' comes over the R/T.

'Red Leader here. Wings yellow and green stay on your targets. Red and blue follow me to 20,000.'

As you obediently begin your climb, you see an Me109 come hurtling out of the clouds, headed directly for you. Make a Pilot skill roll. If you succeed, turn to 254. If you do not, turn to 114.

201

For a second, you lose the Me109 and almost immediately sense danger. Craning your neck around, you can just see the yellow propeller blades of the 109 behind you. Now turn to 143.

202

Taking a last look behind you, you break into a run. Luckily, there is a gully just beyond the bushes into which you can drop. Sprinting along the bottom of it, you finally scramble up a bank some two hundred yards away. There is no sound of pursuit behind you. Looking rapidly around, you try to judge the best way to go next. The wood is more dense here, although there is a patch of rising bare ground off to your right. Will you head deeper into the wood (turn

to **105**) or will you go towards the hill to try to get your bearings (turn to **206**)?

203

Pulling the joystick back, you feel the G-forces mounting as your airplane climbs at maximum. Looking back over your shoulder, you see the Me109 which was tailing you whip by into the clouds. Breathing a sigh of relief, turn to **30**.

204

Was Madeleine one of the casualties? If yes go to **101**. If not hide the bodies of the Germans and dispose of the truck, then go to **71**.

205

You manage to cross the warning wire undetected and creep towards the perimeter fence. Bravely, you stand fully upright to test your theory. The searchlight passes within a couple of feet of you, but the point where you stand is still in darkness. You breathe a sigh of relief.

The return to your hut is made without incident and you collapse into your bunk, your mind racing. To get through the wire, you will need cutters of some kind. After escaping from the camp you should also have a map, or at least a knowledge of the surrounding country. Will you decide to go ahead with the plan on your own and make some wire-cutters (turn to **119**) or will you decide that it is too risky on your own and tell the S.B.O. (turn to **46**)?

206

A few minutes of scrambling succeeds in putting you atop a steep, barren knoll. Making every effort not to be seen, you crawl on your hands and knees along the top of it. Looking down and back the way you have come, you can see the road and the parked truck. Three corpses lie together off to one side whilst the remaining RAF men sit with their hands on their heads, covered by a soldier with a machine gun. The other Germans are nowhere to be seen. You are definitely on your own.

As you rise slightly to get a better view a bullet whizzes past your head. The other Germans have spotted you. Will you surrender (turn to **167**) or will you try to escape their trap (turn to **264**)?

207

The man is stunned to see you. Your distinctive RAF uniform has made him very nervous.

'You are English,' he begins.

'Yes,' you reply. 'I need your help, can you please assist me?'

'Maybe. I know a man in town,' he says.

'What is your name?' you ask.

'Jean,' he replies. 'Here, put on my coat and follow me.'

You both walk confidently out of the goods yard and into the streets of Metz. It is a beautiful city, thankfully not yet damaged by bombing. He gestures to a house on the opposite side of the road. You offer to give back his coat, but he refuses and urges you to hurry. Now go to **165**.

208

After a few more minutes' lung-bursting run, you reach the end of the forest, and the end of your cover. West lies a village, and running north-south a train track. Will you head for the village (go to **56**) or will you decide to jump on the next train that comes along (go to **269**)?

209

The headlight belongs to a motor-bike and side-car, and the occupants have seen you. Make a Luck roll as they open fire with the machine-gun mounted on the side-car. If you succeed, go to **273**. If you fail, go to **141**.

210

The train covered a fair distance while you were sleeping. Feeling rather bedraggled, you struggle to your feet and survey your new surroundings. You are in a railway shunting yard and, straining your eyes, you can just make out a sign – Metz. You are in France!

You climb out of the box-car and look for any signs of life. A railway worker is strolling along further up the track. Will you approach him (go to **207**) or will you head off in the opposite direction (go to **99**)?

211

The vehicle lurches forward as you put it into gear. Bullets graze the metalwork around you and shatter the windscreen. Without stopping, you smash your fist through the starred glass and hurtle down the road with your foot hard on the accelerator. A mile later, you pull over to the side of the road and help the other two escapers from their rubbish cans in the back. Abandoning the vehicle, you decide to split up and head into the woods beside the road. Which way will you go? Towards Belgium (go to **151**) or towards Switzerland (go to **243**)?

212

After pausing for a few seconds at the main gate, the van pulls away again. You wait a few minutes before cautiously lifting the lid of the bin to peer out. Through the wooden slatted sides of the vehicle you can see trees and the road outside the camp. You have made it – so far. Clambering out of the can, you help the other two to extricate themselves and then, one by one, you drop out of the open back of the van. Deciding to split up, you shake hands and take leave of the others. Which way will you go? South-west towards Switzerland (go to **139**) or north-west towards Belgium (go to **152**)?

213

At the last minute you flip the airplane into a barrel roll and manage to avoid the blast. The Germans are turning for home now. Will you follow them at a respectful distance (go to **246**) or will you close with the stragglers (go to **200**)?

214

One of the other Frenchmen has spotted the German. Casually he nudges Eugene, who turns nonchalantly and taps on the window behind him. Looking past him for a moment, you see four men quickly pull a cover over a hole in the floor of the hut and scatter. Another man walks over to the window and chats casually to Eugene until the German has walked past and disappeared.

Eugene turns back to you and smiles. 'As you can see, we are quite busy,' he says. 'Please move away from here.'

Reluctantly, you do so. Now turn to **234**.

215

'I have prisoners. Throw down your weapons!' you scream.

The two guards nearest you obey. After a few seconds, the others follow suit. Herding your hostages forward slightly, you glance into the back of the truck. There are several RAF men inside and, feeling relieved that you have found some reinforcements, you call to them to get out and take the guards' weapons.

As they are doing so, two of the Germans make a

break for it. Instinctively, you squeeze the trigger of your machine-gun and cut them down in mid-run. Now go to 55.

216

Awkwardly, you hit the side of a box-car. Desperately you cling on as the train speeds along. Your arm hurts and feels quite numb – you hope that you have not broken it. Reduce your Agility by 2 until you can get some medical attention. Climbing into the open box-car you check that no one saw you then, pulling the tarpaulin over you, you settle down for the night. Now turn to 210.

217

He ushers you into the kitchen and offers you a seat. Cautiously, you listen to what he has to say, not quite sure whether to believe him or not.

'How can you get me out of Germany?' you ask.

'I drive to France each week to buy produce for my business,' he replies. 'I can hide you tonight, and tomorrow we will drive together to Metz. Then I will take you to a man I know. Perhaps he can get you home.'

Now go to 190.

218

Just as you are reaching up to open the canopy another Spitfire pulls alongside and you recognize the aeroplane of Red Leader.

'Trouble, Thompson?' he asks.

'The old girl's taken a lot of flak,' you reply. 'I think I'll have to bail out.'

'Kite *looks* OK,' he says. 'Stay put and stick close to me. We're following them out.'

Will you stay with Red Leader (turn to **246**) or will you close with the retreating enemy (go to **200**)?

219

The camp seems well-established. As you pass through the first gate you see that it is covered by a tall tower with a machine-gun post at the top. Once inside, you stand in an enclosed parade area which you will soon know as the 'Vorlager'. Looking through the wire into the main camp you can see a large group of prisoners gathering in front of a series of huts inside the compound to welcome you.

Your group is ushered into a building on the left which appears to serve both as a reception centre and a guard barrack room. In turn, the seven of you are searched, then issued with two blankets, washing equipment, a fork, mess-tin and a small packet of tobacco.

Walking with Livermore and Johnson you enter the main compound to be greeted by the rest of the inmates. Instantly, a stream of questions are thrown at you.

' – The Germans haven't landed in England, have they?'

' – Where were you shot down?'

' – How's London getting on?'

With a series of nods and monosyllables you answer the questions without stopping in your walk forward to meet the Senior British Officer.

Group Captain Evans' hut lies in the centre of the British part of the camp and you are led there by a group of other prisoners. Straightening your uniform, you knock on his door. Now turn to **163**.

220

All of you except the first Frenchman are recaptured and given thirty days in the cooler. If this is your third visit to the cooler, turn to **70**. When you get out of solitary confinement, you must decide what to do next. If you have not already worked with John Stallard, turn to **146**. If you have not already worked with Moseby, turn to **259**. If you have worked with both of them before, then turn to **257**.

221

The words stumble out, and the Goon grows suspicious. He shouts for the sergeant of the guard. Your attempt has failed. A month and a half in the cooler this time, and vital equipment confiscated.

If this is your third visit to the cooler, turn to **70**. When you get out of solitary confinement, you must decide what to do next. If you have not already worked with August Dechant, turn to **191**. If you have not already worked with Moseby, turn to **259**. If you have worked with both of them before, then turn to **257**.

222

The fighter banks away to the left and out of your sight. Glancing around, you can see bombers below you. Will you attack them (go to **60**) or will you continue to look for fighters (go to **16**)?

123

223

It takes you several days of construction to make a serviceable pair of wire-cutters from the stolen knives, but finally you manage it. One thing now remains: will you make the attempt on your own, or take someone with you? If you intend to go alone, turn to **253**. If you decide to take someone with you, turn to **115**.

224

Carefully, you creep down the stairs and leave through the back door. You know that to the east lies the forest and beyond that the prison camp. To the west are France, Belgium and Luxembourg. Deciding to head west, you keep to the shadows until you are out of town.

Ahead is a railway track. If you could jump on a train, you would leave Germany behind and be miles away by the morning. You wait for a little while until you see the dimmed lights of a locomotive in the distance. As it approaches you brace yourself to leap on to it. Make a Luck roll. If you succeed, go to **216**. If you fail, go to **48**.

225

Picking up a saucepan you stun the man, then tie him up. Grabbing his rucksack and thrusting as much food into it as you can you head off towards the road. Now go to **116**.

226

The nearest guard kneels down to take off his boot.

Cautiously, you approach to within a few feet; he has still not looked up. Will you kick him (go to **113**) or will you try to grab his gun (go to **87**)?

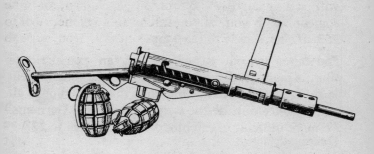

227

The six of you make it to the wire and locate the hole. Unravelling the fuse wire from the places where the wire has been cut, you squeeze through one by one. Then, as the second Frenchman goes through the hole, he slips and makes a heavy sound as he falls. Test your Luck. If you succeed, turn to **268**. If you fail, turn to **53**.

228

You are not sure whether to trust him, but before you can decide on a course of action, he returns.

'I will hide you here until tomorrow,' he says, 'then I will take you across the border in my truck. I go to Metz every week to buy fresh produce. They will not suspect me.'

125

You decide for the moment to play along with the situation. Go to **190**.

229

There is no escape from this, so you decide to surrender. Go to **167**.

230

The other Briton, Reggie Butler, an ex-Hurricane pilot, is made leader. He decides that the attempt will be made in three days' time and that you should all split up once outside the wire, to make the Germans' job more difficult in catching you. Now turn to **227**.

231

The tail of the Me109 disintegrates in your burst of cannon fire. The aircraft breaks up and falls from the sky.

'Thanks, Alistair,' says Roy gratefully.

'Good luck,' you wish him and his crippled aircraft before heading back towards the main dogfight. Now turn to **63**.

232

Grabbing the woodcutter's axe you bury it in his head – the man does not even move. Throwing down the weapon you steal as much food as you can find and then exchange clothes with the dead man. As you leave the hut, go to **156**.

233

Sitting in solitary confinement, you have plenty of time to think. How could the Goons have known

126

about the tunnel? Someone in the camp must have informed.

During the brief exercise periods, you discuss this with your fellow tunnellers and they agree. An inquiry will be held when you all get out.

If this is your third visit to the cooler, turn to **70**. If it is not, go to **2**.

234

You wander off towards your own part of the camp, and spend the rest of the day reading. After Appel, you feel rather tired, despite having done very little today, and you go to bed early.

At about 3.00 A.M., you awake to the sound of sirens blaring. For a moment, you almost believe that you are back in London, listening to an air-raid warning. You start to panic, remembering that the camp has no air-raid shelters.

'Someone's trying to escape,' comments the man in the next bunk excitedly as he clambers down.

Will you stay in your own bunk and ignore the excitement (go to **78**) or will you get up and have a look outside (go to **125**).

235

You walk off slowly, pretending to find somewhere private in which you can answer the call of nature. As you walk, you note that the nearest guard is eyeing you suspiciously, but he does nothing to stop you. Reaching some bushes, will you decide to run (turn to **202**) or, realizing your attempt would end in failure, will you simply use them as a toilet before returning (turn to **272**)?

'There are nine towers, with searchlights and a constantly manned machine-gun in each,' is the reply when you ask about the prison. 'Then there are about half-a-dozen dog handlers and thirty or so other guards, plus the Ferrets, of course.'

'Ferrets?' you ask.

'Yes. The Abwehr men. They just snoop about looking for anything suspicious.'

'Where are we, exactly?' you inquire.

'About twenty-five miles from Frankfurt, near the Rhine Valley. It's about a hundred and fifty miles to the Swiss border. Thinking of escaping?' someone asks with a grin.

If you are not sure about giving any information away, you can avoid this question by asking one of your own (turn to **237**). On the other hand, if you want to find out about any attempts in progress, you could ask him if the camp has an Escape Committee and turn to **293**.

237

'How many have managed to escape from here?' you ask an airman beside you at the table.

'Not many. Six, I think. The French try it all the time, but most of them get caught. They're good tunnellers, though,' he replies.

Will you ask if there is an Escape Committee (go to **293**) or will you decide to try to escape on your own (go to **149**)?

238

Make an Agility skill roll. If you succeed, turn to **142**. If you do not, turn to **136**.

239

The waiter nods his approval and disappears for five minutes. He returns with a plate of sausages, bread and coffee, wishes you 'bon appetit' and saunters off again. Now turn to **283**.

240

Walking towards the huts, you see a group of French prisoners loitering around in front of one particular building. They look pretty suspicious. You decide that they must be up to something – planning an escape, perhaps. Curiosity turns your steps towards them. If you wish to try talking to one of the Frenchmen, make a Language skill roll. If you succeed, go to **270**, if not, go to **252**. If you decide to ignore them, then turn to **234**.

241

After a cursory look they decide that they were mistaken, and remount. With a last brief glance they roar off into the distance, northwards.

You let them get out of sight, then cross the road and head south. Presently, you see a train track running parallel to your route. This is exactly what you have been looking for, a fast way out of the area. You decide to wait for the next one to come along, and jump on. Now go to **269**.

242

You decide not to cross the road, and are glad you didn't as seconds later a motor-bike and side-car speeds past, with two German soldiers on it. A

RW
86

moment later the road is no longer visible and you are once more in the semi-darkness of the forest.

The baying is getting even nearer now. Will you run (go to **208**) or just quicken your pace (go to **287**)?

243

As the sirens begin to wail and the tannoys bark out commands to the guards, you slip away into the forest. Your sense of triumph is coupled with your fear, as you hear the howl of the guard-dogs not far behind you. Without looking back you crash blindly through the undergrowth until you reach a tarmac road. There seems to be nothing moving along it. Will you cross the road (go to **52**) or will you follow the road west, still keeping to the forest (go to **121**)?

244

You recount your exploits over the Channel and at the end of your statement he seems satisfied enough by your explanations.

'I am glad that you have chosen to cooperate, Thompson. I see no need for any further unpleasantness. You will be taken to Luftwaffe headquarters – they are responsible for downed RAF pilots. Goodbye.'

A Kubelwagon staff car is parked outside with three armed men in it and you are swiftly driven away to Luftwaffe HQ. Now turn to **256**.

245

You follow the corridor for a few dozen metres before reaching a doorway on your right. Ahead, the corridor continues round a corner beyond the doorway. Will you try the door (turn to **104**) or will you continue along the corridor (turn to **19**)?

246

The German bombers are slowly pulling away from you, their remaining fighter escort desperately trying to fend off the pursuing Spitfires.

'Red Leader, Red Leader, new formation of bandits heading our way. Estimate fifty – all fighters!' comes over the R/T.

'Red Leader here. Wings yellow and green stay on your targets. Red and blue follow me to 20,000.'

'Red Four here, Leader,' you transmit. 'May have a problém staying with you.'

'See what you can do, Red Four,' comes the reply.

Gradually, you make the climb to 20,000 feet. About a mile away you see the new formation of Me109s peel away from their tight grouping and fall on green and yellow wings.

Checking your controls cautiously, you prepare to attack.

'Red Leader here. Green and yellow wings, break now. Red and blue, tally ho!' comes the order.

Now turn to **63**.

247

You cannot pull up in time and your Spitfire is caught in the ball of flame. Great bursts of fire wash over the front of your aircraft. You realize that your only chance is to bail out. Ripping at the canopy, make a Luck roll. If you succeed, go to **280**. If you do not, go to **74**.

248

Make an Agility skill roll. If you succeed, go to **181**. If you fail, go to **166**.

249

Behind you, you can hear another vehicle getting closer. The truck has stopped near the copse and several Germans jump from the back of it. Will you make a dash for it (go to **141**) or will you surrender (go to **37**)?

250

The machine-gun fire is getting more accurate by the second and before you have a chance to rethink your decision, you feel a searing pain as a burst of fire rips through your chest. You fall to the floor, mortally wounded.

Your adventure ends here.

251

Both Germans have their backs to you. Holding the

rifle securely in both hands, you sprint towards the cab of the truck. As you reach it, you see three other Germans standing waiting for something a few yards off. Leaping into the cab, you shove the truck into gear. Make a Driving skill roll. If you succeed, turn to **15**. If not, turn to **120**.

252

The Frenchmen obviously don't understand you – your grasp of the language is not good enough. It seems that they don't want people hanging around here anyway, because they gesture to you to move off. Now turn to **234**.

253

You cannot wait to make sure that you pick the right person so, having made up your mind to go on your own, you decide to go tonight. At about midnight, when everyone else in your hut is asleep, you carefully open the window and slip out.

Creeping slowly across the compound you watch the guards and the searchlight beams. When all looks clear, you make your dash towards the wire. Stepping over the warning wire you begin to cut through the fence. The thickness of the wire means that you will have to spend quite some time at it, and each second you spend crouched in the darkness takes years off your life! But, finally, you manage to cut a gap large enough to squeeze through. Make a Luck roll. If you succeed, turn to **90**. If you fail, turn to **98**.

254

Throttling back, you watch as the Me109 overshoots

above you. Pulling back on the stick, you squeeze off a short burst and riddle the 109's cockpit. Instantly, it plunges into a dive and you sideslip to avoid it. You must have hit the pilot.

You watch your victim descend towards the Channel for a few moments before banking around and heading for the main dogfight. Now turn to **63**.

255

As you re-emerge from the undergrowth you can see that three of your comrades were not as lucky as you. Even now, the Germans are dragging their bodies away into the brush.

One German seems slightly hurt and they are all very angry as they herd you and your remaining colleagues back into the truck. Now turn to **47**.

256

The town is full of soldiers. The Germans seem to have preparations well under way for their invasion of England. You wish you were still in the skies defending your homeland against them and you curse yourself for the mistake which has brought you here.

Presently, you arrive at Luftwaffe HQ and are locked in a cell for the night. At daybreak a guard arrives with a bowl of food and a mug of coffee; he does not speak English. Will you use your Language skill to try to talk to him (go to **140**) or will you stay quiet and eat, hoping for an opportunity to get away later (go to **160**)?

257

Having tried virtually every means of escape from the

camp, you are utterly dispirited and depressed. You resolve to sit out the war in peace inside this Stalag Luft. It seems pointless to try anything else when all has failed. The Germans have beaten you and there is nothing for it but to forget any more escape attempts.

Your adventure ends here.

258

The man says, 'Come with me, I am French. You can trust me.'

You look at him for a moment, then rise and follow him to the kitchen. Now go to **188**.

259

You are introduced to Frank 'Mole' Moseby, the 'Tunnel King', a jovial Yorkshireman in his late thirties.

'I'm a hard taskmaster, Mr Thompson,' he says. Do your bit, though, and I'll see you right.'

He details you to start shift work in the current tunnel. Now go to **299**.

260

As you reach the warning wire, a searchlight catches you in its beam.

'Halte! Hande hoch!' a loud German voice commands.

You freeze on the spot. There is no point in being a hero with nowhere to run to. Reluctantly, you stand still as the sirens wail in your ears. Within seconds, a group of guards arrive and march you off to the cooler.

'There is a standard one week of solitary for the

first offence,' explains the German duty officer. 'Basic rations and half an hour of exercise per day.'

Now turn to **31**.

261

He does not understand your stumbling German and shrugs before turning to leave. Will you attack him (turn to **238**) or wait for a better chance later (turn to **29**)?

262

Several more minutes pass and the plane disappears from view, heading west. About a quarter of a mile away you see a truck making its way along a dirt road towards you. Will you stay put (go to **249**) or will you run (go to **5**)?

263

You barely understand him and panic. Shoving the man over the barrier, you swing your arm around and catch one of the soldiers on the chin. He collides with the other two and in seconds the four men are on the ground. Seizing your chance you grab Madeleine by the hand and run through the gate.

Make a Luck roll. If you succeed, go to **196**. If you fail, go to **122**.

264

A sudden burst of gunfire from behind sends you instinctively face down on the ground. Looking up cautiously, you can see a lone German standing some twenty yards away. Will you surrender (go to **167**) or will you keep still, hoping he will think he has killed you, and then try to escape (go to **93**)?

265

Desperately, you come up with a plan. As the Germans approach, you pretend to cower away in fear. Crouching on the ground and wrapping your arms over your head, you pretend that you have finally gone over the edge – 'Wire Happy', they call it in the camp.

'Don't touch me!' you scream. 'I can't stand it! I can't stand it! Don't touch me! I can't live here anymore!'

Despite your act, the Goons know something is up. Ignoring your act, one holds you at gun-point while the other two head straight for the hut.

You hear muffled, raised voices, and minutes later three grimy figures emerge under arrest.

You and your comrades are given a month in the cooler, and the tunnel is filled in. Now go to **233**.

266

The man is Swiss, although he speaks fluent German; a lot of Swiss do. He is under orders to escort all escapees to the local officials. He explains that you will be interned and held for a while, until the British Embassy can organize the necessary visas and transport details.

You are now a free man. Congratulations! You will see Great Britain again, and eventually return to the cockpit of an RAF plane to fly once more.

Your adventure ends here.

Where am I to be taken?' you ask.

'Stalag Luft 14. A new camp inside the borders of the Fatherland,' he replies.

You thank him and he turns away to leave the cell. Now that you are rested, you are feeling stronger. Will you attack him now (turn to **238**) or wait for a better chance later (turn to **29**)?

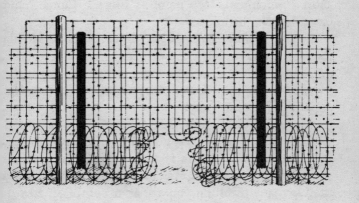

268

Quickly you cross the open ground between the camp and the forest. Once inside the shelter of the trees, you decide to split up. Good wishes are exchanged quickly, and you are soon left alone. Which way will you go? Will you head south-west towards Switzerland (go to **139**) or north-west towards Belgium (go to **152**)?

269

You do not have long to wait. A train looms out of

the night hurtling south. As it approaches, you brac
yourself, ready to jump.

Make a Luck roll as you hurl yourself towards
handrail. If you succeed, go to **216**. If you fail, go to
48.

270

'We are keeping an eye on the Goons,' explains a
short Frenchman. 'My name is Eugene Lange, chie
Goon-baiter,' he jokes.

'I am Alistair Thompson, chief Nothing at the
moment,' you reply.

'You have not been here long, then,' he says with a
twinkle in his eye. 'But perhaps you will get enough
excitement soon.'

You shrug and look past him at the compound
Only a few yards away, around the corner of a
hut, one of the Ferrets is approaching the German
snoopers. If you wish to try to warn Eugene, and risk
the Germans thinking you are an accomplice, turn to
298. If you think it would be safer to do nothing
turn to **214**.

271

The truck rattles along the rutted road and finally
comes to a halt. You hear the cab doors slam shut
and voices slowly disappearing into the distance.
Cautiously you poke your head out of the canvas and
look around. You are in the goods yard of a railway
station. The sign says Ludwigshafen, a town you
know to be at the north of the Rhine valley, still deep
in Germany. The French border is some thirty or so

miles away, and far to the south, over a hundred miles distant, is Switzerland.

Trains must leave here bound for either destination. You leave the truck and search for a suitable train. Eventually you find one of each. Which one will you take? The French one (go to **128**) or the Swiss one (go to **180**)?

272

All of a sudden, one of the other prisoners makes a break for it. Within seconds, the others have done the same, fanning out in several directions. The guard yells and then fires. Instinctively, you run also. There is a gully just beyond the bushes into which you can drop. Sprinting along the bottom of it, you finally scramble up a bank some two hundred metres away. There is no sound of pursuit behind you. Looking rapidly around you try to judge the best way to go next. The wood is more dense here, although there is a patch of rising bare ground off to your right. Will you head deeper into the wood (turn to **105**) or will you go towards the hill to try to get your bearings (turn to **206**)?

273

You manage to avoid the burst of machine-gun fire and run off into the field on the other side of the road. Luckily there are no gates nearby, so the combination cannot follow you. They fire off a desultory volley at you and then roar off to the north.

Without pausing for breath you continue your run. Ahead is a train track. Following the line south, you

decide to jump on to the next train that comes along.
Now go to **269**.

274

The guard levels his rifle and fires. The shot hits you
squarely in the chest and you fall choking to the
forest floor.

Your adventure ends here.

275

The Germans recognize the truck as it reaches the
road-block. Georges gets out and walks over to the
soldiers. From the little you can hear and understand
he tells them that he thinks he saw a man running
across country about ten miles back, heading for
Luxembourg. They thank him, and radio the sighting
to their headquarters. Georges bids them farewell,
returns to the truck and restarts the engine. The
Germans clear a path for him and wave him through.
They did not even ask to see his pass!

'They are looking for an escaped POW, but we
have not seen one, have we, Brother?' he laughs. 'I
told them that I saw someone running through the
fields; they believed me.'

Now go to **127**.

276

Georges chats incessantly throughout the journey;
despite the fact that he thinks all will be well, he is
obviously nervous. He explains that he has little
difficulty in obtaining transit permission from the local
commander as he visits Henri's restaurant regularly.

There are very few German soldiers visible on the

roads, but as you reach Birkenfeld some thirty miles from the border, you see a road-block up ahead.

Will you decide to go along with Georges' plan and pretend to be asleep (go to **275**) or will you try to make a dash for it (go to **134**)?

277

As the E-boat pulls alongside your dinghy you see your enemy at close quarters for the first time. One German mans the heavy machine-gun at the rear of the boat, pointing it at you; three others stand ready to haul you aboard.

The largest of the three, obviously an officer, says, 'RAF kaput!' and, nodding, you agree. You are finished; for now, anyway. With the help of the Germans you struggle aboard and are given a blanket and a steaming mug of coffee. You settle down in the relative warmth of the forward cabin and almost at once fall asleep. Now turn to **86**.

278

You spend the rest of the day pondering the possibilities. Afternoon Appel comes and goes and finally you are locked up for the night.

Waiting until about 9.00 P.M., you carefully get out of your bunk and gently prise open the window nearest the bed. It opens fairly easily, and you slip out into the darkness. The night is illuminated only by the steady sweep of the searchlight fanning across the camp. Test your Luck as you dash across the open ground to the warning wire. If you succeed, go to **205**. If not, go to **260**.

'Madeleine,' you say, 'where are we? At Paris yet?'

'Almost, Emile, my brother,' she insists.

'Ah good, and who is this?' you ask.

'A German officer, Emile, he would like to take me to the theatre, at the weekend,' she replies.

The German smiles and nods.

'But what about Phillippe, your husband? He would not take kindly to that, being in the French government,' you lie.

The German's face goes red. He is obviously a little worried now.

'I have some important papers to sign, would you excuse me, please. I am sorry to have troubled you,' he says.

'Of course. Goodbye,' you reply, almost in unison.

Breathing a sigh of relief you sit up, determined not to fall asleep again. Protectively you place your arm around Madeleine and decide that you must pretend to everyone that you are husband and wife. It will be safer. Now go to **51**.

280

As you heave yourself out of the cockpit of your burning Spitfire, the sudden blast of air whips you out and away from the aircraft.

You count as you fall, then pull the ripcord of your parachute. The oil from the fire has covered your goggles and you push them up on to your forehead after the chute has opened. You are still rubbing your eyes as you hit the water.

The channel is calm and not too cold. You unharness your chute and kick off your heavy flying boots.

Struggling free of the lines of the chute you get your rubber dinghy inflated and, exhausted, heave yourself into it. Now turn to **34**.

281

Keeping to the edge of the woods you see a steady stream of traffic, all military and heading west. Perhaps there is a railway depot nearby. The trucks do not appear to have anyone in the back, just three men in the cab. As the next one passes you leap on to it and hide behind some ammunition boxes. Now go to **271**.

282

One of your prisoners shouts 'Achtung!' and the two Germans at the rear of the truck spin round. What will you do? Open fire (go to **112**) or command them to surrender (go to **215**)?

283

You wolf down the food. It is the best you have ever eaten. Proper food after weeks of turnips and ersatz coffee, that foul liquid the Germans use in place of real coffee.

It dawns on you that you cannot pay. You will have to try to make a break for it. Now go to **133**.

284

You head off across the open fields towards the west. The countryside is very quiet with no sound of traffic. On the first night you cover about twelve miles, not as far as you had hoped and, exhausted, begin to search for somewhere to sleep.

About two miles ahead is a small copse. Quickening your pace as the sun begins to rise you make for it.

Suddenly overhead you hear the humming of an aircraft engine and, looking up, see a Storch spotter plane. The pilot has sighted you. Luckily there is nowhere for him to land, but no doubt he has radioed your position to his base. Breaking into a run you head for the cover of the trees. Several minutes later, with the aircraft still buzzing overhead, you dive into the wood.

What will you do now? Stay put (go to **262**) or continue westwards (go to **5**)?

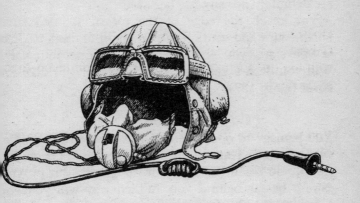

285

Snatching at the lid of your rubbish can, you hurl it at the guard and manage to knock the rifle from his hands. Will you make for the cab of the van (go to **100**) or will you run out of the main gate (go to **81**)?

286

After you have gone only a few paces you find the

corridor is blocked by a door. Opening it, you find yourself in a yard. A truck stands in the centre of the yard with its engine running, and there are two German guards at the rear of the vehicle. Checking your rifle and releasing the safety catch, you must decide whether to fire at the two Germans (go to **42**), make a run for the truck and hope to drive away in it (go to **251**) or return inside and see where the other branch of the corridor leads (go to **245**).

287

The pursuers seem not to be getting any closer, but are definitely not any further away.

You reach the edge of the forest. A road runs north-south and cautiously you begin to cross it. Just as you start, you see a headlight coming your way. Will you dash across (go to **209**) or will you dive for cover (go to **187**)?

288

You manage to open a hole and squeeze through the wire. Sprinting across the dead ground outside the camp, you reach the safety of the forest. But pursuit cannot be far behind you. Which way will you go? North-west towards Belgium (turn to **151**) or south-west towards Switzerland (turn to **243**)?

289

The rest of the journey is largely uneventful. Each night, your guards lock you up in a local jail and by day they handcuff you to the seats in the truck. Eventually, you arrive late one afternoon at Stalag Luft 14, near Wiesbaden in Germany. The soldiers from the truck hand you over to the prison guards before driving away. Now turn to **219**.

290

A bullet misses your head by a hair's breadth, but in seconds you are safely in the forest. Pursuit will not be far behind and you must decide quickly: will you head south-west towards Switzerland (go to **243**) or north-west towards Belgium (go to **151**)?

291

As you pass through the gate, the guard retrieves his rifle. Instinctively, you try to dodge, but the range is too short for a reasonable shot to miss.

The bullet hits you squarely in the back and you drop to the ground, mortally wounded. At least you did not die within the confines of the camp.

Your adventure ends here.

292

Your reasoned arguments and obvious honesty seem to make an impression upon the senior officers.

'But if Thompson did not inform the Goons, then who did?' asks a Belgian.

Suspicion now naturally falls upon the other recent arrivals at the camp, and the officers question you searchingly about them. You tell what little you know, but cannot think that it will help very much.

Then, suddenly, you remember a conversation which you had several weeks earlier with Flight Lieutenant Parkinson. You had been talking about London and happened to mention the air-raid shelter outside the Armed Services Club in Piccadilly. His

ply had been vague and you got the impression that
e didn't know what you were talking about. But he
ad told you that he was stationed at Hornchurch,
ust outside London. It seems a bit strange that he
ould not have been into the West End on leave, and
he first stopping point for every pilot was always the
Armed Services Club.

You voice your suspicions to the assembled officers
nd they decide to question Parkinson.

Now turn to **40**.

293

I suppose if I'm thinking about escape, I should talk
o the Escape Committee,' you say. 'Is there one in
his camp?'

'I'm not sure that I can tell you that,' he replies.
After all, you haven't been here long and we don't
know you yet. I'm sure they'll let you know soon,' he
eplies.

Thanking him for the information, you get up and
eave, deciding to have a look around. Now go to
49.

294

You have no choice but to try to escape. Now go to
07.

295

After a few minutes' walk you arrive at the E-boat
command HQ and are ushered into the commander's
office for interrogation. A bald, portly man of indefi-
nable rank sits at a desk, partially hidden by mounds
of paperwork. As you enter, he sits up.

'Ah, RAF?'

'Yes,' you reply, standing to attention.

'Your name, rank and serial number?'

'67524 Flight Officer Alistair Thompson, sir!'

'You were seen shooting at a German pilot who ha bailed out, Flight Officer. What do you have to sa for yourself?'

Shocked at this lie, will you simply repeat you name, rank and serial number (go to **198**) or will yo deny it and give an account of your actions over th Channel (go to **244**)?

296

Your sentence in the cooler is sixty days. If this your third visit, turn to **70**. When you get out solitary confinement, you must decide what to d next. If you have not already worked with Augu Dechant, turn to **191**. If you have not already worke with Moseby, turn to **259**. If you have worked wit both of them before, then turn to **257**.

297

'I would prefer not to, my husband is a very jealou man,' says Madeleine.

'Of course he would be. So would I, for you ar very beautiful,' replies the German.

Deciding that you really must help her, go to **279**.

298

Being careful not to arouse any suspicion, you nudg Eugene and gesture with your eyes.

He turns nonchalantly and taps on the windo behind him. Looking past him for a moment, you se

ur men quickly pull a cover over a hole in the floor
f the hut and scatter. Another man walks over to the
indow and chats casually to Eugene until the German
as walked past and disappeared.

Eugene turns to you and smiles. 'Thank you for
he warning,' he says. 'That was quick thinking. So
ou want something useful to do? Let me introduce
ou to the Escape Committee. Perhaps they will be
ble to find you something.' Now turn to **145**.

299

The tunnel leaves from the store hut by the kitchen
nd runs due west, hopefully to the tree line beyond
he cleared ground outside the camp. You soon settle
nto a daily routine of digging for two shifts of two
ours each. By the third week, you have grown used
o the claustrophobic conditions in the tunnel.

Digging at the face one morning, you remove a
arge rock which is blocking your way but, as you do
o, the roof of the tunnel caves in. You must test
our Luck. If you succeed, turn to **153**. If not, turn
o **9**.

300

Make a Firearm skill roll. If you succeed, you kill
ne German if you threw an odd number, and two if
you threw an even number. You must now throw for
he rest of the group:

Madeleine	Firearm Skill 7
Edouard	Firearm Skill 8
Maurice	Firearm Skill 6
Bertrand	Firearm Skill 7

| Driver | Firearm Skill 8 |
| Ebonar | Firearm Skill 9 |

The same applies for all the members of the resistance, an odd number kills one German, an even kills two. When you have thrown for all the above, the remaining Germans will fire back. Eliminate the Germans in the order they are below:

Sergeant	Firearm Skill 8
Corporal	Firearm Skill 7
Private	Firearm Skill 7
Private	Firearm Skill 6
Private	Firearm Skill 6
Private	Firearm Skill 5
Private	Firearm Skill 5
Private	Firearm Skill 6
Captain	Firearm Skill 8

When the Germans fire, the first will fire at you, then in turn they will fire down the list of resistance people. If you are killed, or all of your resistance companions are killed, your adventure ends here. If you win, go to **204**.